9,000 Hours
and Counting

A Pilot's Log

9,000 Hours
and Counting

A Pilot's Log

Ibu Alvarado

Cecropia Press

cecropiapress.com

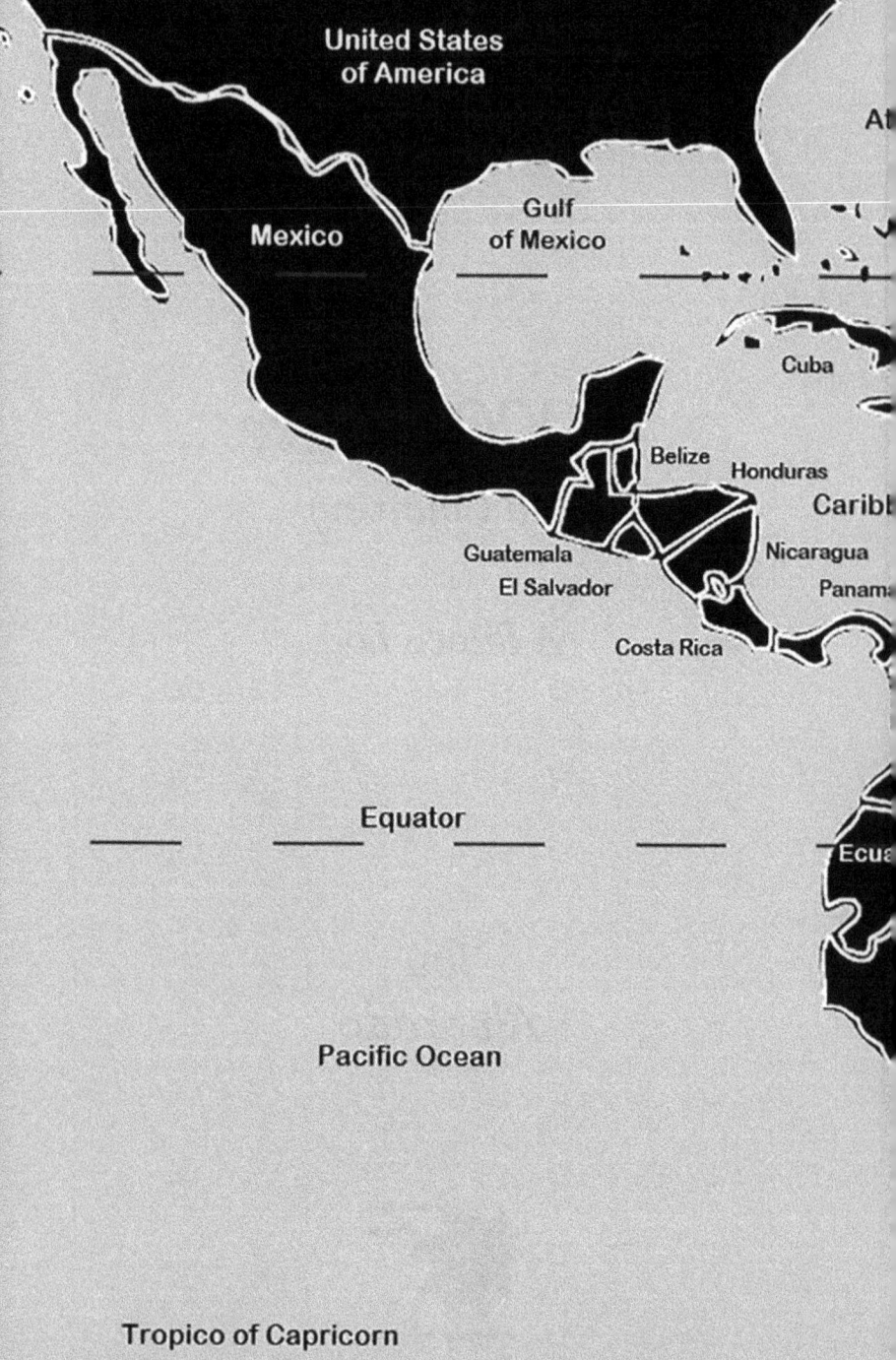

Copyright © 2018, Luis Alonso Alvarado Kinkead
All Right Reserved.

920.71
AL76 Alvarado Kinkead, Luis Alonso
        9000 Hours and Counting : A pilot's
Log / Luis Alonso Alvarado K. ; traductor
  Teófilo J. Alvarado Veazey -- Panamá :
Cecropia Press, 2018.
            344p. ; 21 cm.

  ISBN 978-9962-715-14-6 (Tapa suave)
  ISBN 978-9962-715-15-3 (eBook)

  1. BIOGRAPHIES
  2. PANAMA – BIOGRAPHIES
  3. AVIATION - PANAMA
  4. AVIATION – PANAMA - HISTORY   I. Title.

Cecropia Press

cecropiapress.com

*For Guille Palm and Jimmy Smith.
Aviators, friends, always remembered.*

Contents

Glossary	*13*
Prologue	*15*
Part 1 - Background	*19*
1 First Memories	21
2 A World Apart	27
3 El Campo	29
4 Airport Recollections	33
Part 2 - The Beginning	*41*
5 Aeronautical Development	43
6 Aerial Spraying	45
7 Changuinola Loyalty	49
Part 3 - Initiation	*61*
8 The Bug Bites	63
9 Pheromones Aloft	73
10 Formal Instruction	82
Part 4 - Licensed Pilot	*91*
11 Learning by Doing	93
12 Exotic Species	95
13 Get-home-itis	100
14 Unconventional Check Airman	105
15 Back Seat Jockey	107
16 Cloud Seeding	111
17 Splashdown in Nargana	117
Part 5 - The Remarkable 180	*129*
18 Rebirth of a Classic	131
19 The Yellow Fever	135
20 Flight of Uncertainty	139
21 Vital Oxygen	143
22 Possessed by the Devil	145
23 Farewell to a Friend	149

Part 6 - The Maule	155
24 The Reluctant Missionary	157
25 Rescued	162
26 A Prolonged Restoration	165
27 In the Air Again	168
28 Erratic Behavior	173
29 Hindered	176
30 Back on Track	180
31 Energized Plane and Pilot	185
32 Duty Fulfilled	197
Part 7 - Aero Perlas	209
33 One More Rung	211
34 Captain's Stripes	215
35 Stressful Routine	222
Part 8 - Evergreen International Airlines	231
36 Recruitment and Training	233
37 Getting Acclimatized	240
38 Woes of the Captaincy	247
39 Mexican Stopover	253
40 Mission Rejected	258
41 End of a Saga	260
Part 9 - Adrenaline Overdose	269
42 Allure of Adventure	271
43 Unexpected Layover	277
44 Puerto Leguizamo	286
45 Jungle Haven	290
46 Acceptance and Determination	299
47 Distorted New Year	305
48 End of a Nightmare	311
Epilogue	321
Notes	323
Books about Aviation in Panama	337
Acknowledgments	339
The Aviator	341

Glossary
Aviation Jargon

Abort	Action taken by the pilot to discontinue or reject a takeoff.
Breaking on top	To ascend through a layer of clouds to a clear sky above.
Briefing	Verbal plan given by the pilot flying to the crew that describes the actions each will take in case of a failure during takeoff.
Check Ride	Examination of a pilot's competence in a specific aircraft.
Clean the plane	To retract the extended flaps to the neutral position, 0°.
Flaps	Downstream extensions of the wings that serve to increase the lift at low airspeeds.
Floating	Flying over the runway during a landing without being able to touch down.
Ground Loop	To lose control of the airplane on the ground resulting in a horizontal rotation.
Grounded	Aircraft or crewmember restricted from flying for technical, legal or medical reasons.
Hanging by the prop	Airplane whose wings barely maintain lift subject to propeller revolutions.
Hot Landing	Landing with too much speed.

Missed Approach	To discontinue an approach to landing.
Overhaul	To completely recondition or replace all internal moving parts of an engine.
Scud running	Flying and looking for openings in the clouds while trying to stay in visual conditions.
Side Slip	Sliding through the air with crossed controls increasing the descent rate in order to lose height while maintaining airspeed. Maneuver used to make a normal landing during a too high approach.
Stall	Loss of lift of the wing due to low airspeed and exaggerated angle of attack preventing flight.

Prologue

As we reach our assigned cruising altitude for this flight, 15,000 feet above mean sea level (msl), I pull back on the engine torques and ask the copilot to adjust the RPMs on the props for cruise flight. We have on our oxygen masks since this is not a pressurized aircraft and regulations require crewmembers to use supplementary oxygen after 30 minutes above 10,000 feet at night. There's not much air traffic and the conversations between airplanes and ground controllers are sporadic on this portion of the flight. It's past 9 p.m. and I'm in command of a Spanish-built turboprop aircraft, a Casa 212 – 200. Tonight we're en route from the Caribbean city of Santa Marta to Bogota, Colombia. The stars are bright on this clear night. Ahead and below I make out the lights of all the town sites along the Magdalena River, one of the most emblematic of South America that traverses 310 miles of Colombian territory. In a few minutes we'll be flying over Barrancabermeja, a mandatory reporting point on this route. I estimate our arrival in Bogota a little before 11 p.m., barely meeting the service time restrictions for crewmembers on this type of flight, an unscheduled on-demand operation. I ask JB, my copilot, to take over flying while I start filling out the company logbook, which requires information on takeoff time, engine performance and settings, altitude, airspeed and groundspeed, as well as cargo and passengers on board. I'm supposed to be carrying a team of health specialist from the U.S. Embassy in Colombia made up of doctors, dentists and veterinarians. They may well be professionals in the field they're identified as, but I know they're also members of the US Army Special Forces. The cockpit conversation is non-existent and might be because we're tired. This trip originated in Liberia, Costa Rica, and we didn't know at the time that once we reached Panama, we would have time only to fuel up and fly on to Santa Marta to comply with this mission. However, I feel at ease and content. On this clear night, from the cockpit, as I admire the immensity of the universe, I'm convinced things shouldn't ever be taken for granted, especially moments such as this. It's a sensation that I know will stay with me for the rest of my life. But how is it that I'm up here flying this airplane on such a spectacular night, and on top of that getting paid to do it? Where did it all begin and how did it come about? Who were the protagonists that helped me get here? That night, May 8, 2007, was when I decided to share my experiences of this passion for flight that I've had since I can remember. What's written here is in, one way or another, an expression of gratitude to those who were crucial in my being able to fulfill this passion for flying. I want to make it clear that I don't pretend this to be a novel with a chronological sequence. Instead it's a compilation of situations that I lived as a pilot, as a passenger, or simply as an awed bystander in the aviation environment. One cannot be too stringent as far as exact dates except when I've been able to rely on my flight logbook or on my little red book in which all my aeronautical memories have been registered from the beginning. Both reflect exactly the "where" and "when" but only my red book contains the "how" and "why." The language that I've used is generic but without steering away totally from the technical terminology that is used in every flight. And lastly, this writing is not about the life of an intrepid aviator with exceptional situations but simply the life experiences of someone who has been overcome by aviation. And it all began in Changuinola, in the banana region of the Bocas del Toro province, in the Republic of Panama.

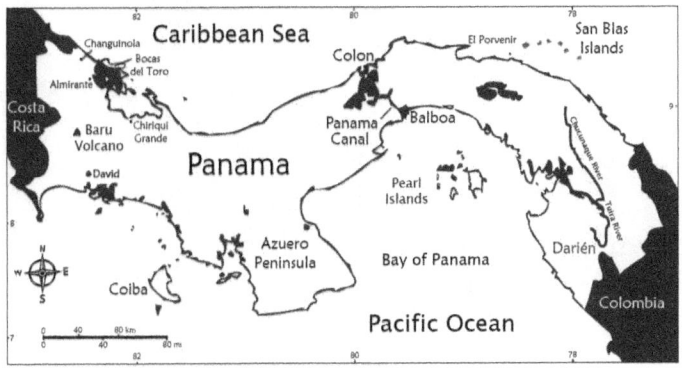

Part 1
Background

1 First Memories
2 A World Apart
3 El Campo
4 Airport Recollections

Chapter 1
First Memories

My first memories of airplanes are hearing the rumble of the DC-3s flying above my house in Farm 8. They were ascending at climb power, heading south towards the Cordillera, Panama's central mountain range. Their departure point: Changuinola, their destination: David. Whatever I was doing, I'd stop and imagine myself flying them. Those are vague memories. But one trip in particular is clearly etched in my mind because two incidents of note occurred, and it's probably why I was hypnotized by flying.

On that occasion, I was accompanying my mother from Sixaola, on the Costa Rican-Panamanian border, to San Jose, Costa Rica, via Puerto Limon. That day I was witness to two in-flight events that could have been pre-destined, something not anticipated nor expected, much less by a five-year-old passenger. It wasn't until many years later that I understood what actually happened on those flights that day. The peculiarity about it all was the positive impact that these events had on me in regards to aviation; a negative effect would have been more reasonable.

In those days, to get from Changuinola to Sixaola one had to travel by a rail motorcar. At the Costa Rica side of the border, the mode of transport shifted to a flat bed on rails. It had benches to sit on and was drawn by a mule to the pasture used as an airstrip by Aerolíneas Vanolli, the mode of travel to Puerto Limon. The plane was a 4-seat single-engine Cessna 170. Once in Puerto

Limon, passengers then transferred to a Líneas Aéreas Costaricenses S.A. (Lacsa) DC-3 for the flight to San Jose. Vanolli, the pilot and owner of the small airline, was a charismatic individual, talkative and with a good sense of humor. He struck a figure with his well-worn pilot's kepis, white shirt with short sleeves rolled up almost to the shoulders, a knife pouch on his belt, Ray-Ban aviator glasses and *Turrialbas*, mid-ankle leather boots with straps, very popular in those years. The airline consisted of only one airplane, that Cessna 170, only one pilot and probably one mechanic, himself. That day we were three passengers, a sewing machine, luggage and several burlap bags full of dried cacao beans. The pasture/landing strip bordered the Sixaola River on Finca Costa Rica, where the United Fruit Company (UFCo) grew cacao for export.

A short dirt track from the wheels of many landings and takeoffs marked the middle of the long pasture. I was in the back seat with my mother where I could observe Vanolli perform his ritual. Once he started the engine and tested the magnetos, I remember watching as he reverently touched a plastic figurine of the Virgin Mary glued on the instrument panel. As the 170 accelerated on the takeoff run, and the tail-wheel began to lift off the ground, I was able to see the end of the track swiftly approaching. At the very end, Vanolli reached down and pulled a lever that was on the floor on the right side of his seat. The plane suddenly ballooned and flew a few feet above the ground for a considerable distance before he gradually lowered the lever and began a slow ascent. That takeoff maneuver was a typical Vanolli takeoff out of that strip. It was not until years later, after I had learned to fly and absorbed the tricks used by local bush pilots, that I understood what he had done: He was applying a routine practice used by pilots operating from short strips based on the ground effect phenomenon.[1-A] This operation, although not in the airplane operating manual, is proven and effective but depends on an important factor: There must be no obstructions in front of the flight trajectory. The Sixaola landing strip fulfilled that requirement.

That morning, after takeoff, and once established on a climb, Vanolli made his way to the coast and leveled the 170 at an altitude of about 1,500 feet. A dark curtain of rain loomed far off in the distance throughout our route. After observing this for a moment, Vanolli then turned west, inland, where the precipitation looked lighter. To the east was the Caribbean Sea, which, although unobstructed, would actually lead us away from our destination. The 170 on that flight must have had what was basic navigation instrumentation for those days, an Automatic Direction Finder (ADF) whose needle points to the radio beacon or station to which it's tuned, usually an AM commercial radio station. After several minutes of trying to find a gap through the rain, Vanolli descended to about 200 feet. He penetrated the rain curtain, and everything darkened. Horizontal visibility was drastically reduced, and only the ground could be distinguished below the wing, barely. At one point Vanolli started to open the window on his side, I assume to try to see straight down by sticking his head out, but we got completely soaked in a matter of seconds, and he quickly closed it back. A few moments after that, I recall the engine stuttering and shaking. Vanolli frantically started pulling and pushing some of the instrument panel's control levers. I don't remember feeling fear or panic, I must have, but what I do remember is that we were all silent, including Vanolli. Although the shaking normalized, and the engine stopped coughing, at times it shuddered as if it might quit, and Vanolli would repeat what he had done before to get it to operate normally. Then he began turning left and right as if in an S trajectory over the ground and looking straight down for a familiar place to orient himself.

"There it is!" I remember having heard him exclaim, a look of relief immediately on his face. It was a railroad track. We flew low for a few more minutes following the railroad on our left and suddenly a clearing appeared. Vanolli circled and aligned the plane to land in what looked like another pasture: Siquirres, another UFCo cacao farm.

As with the takeoff maneuver, it wasn't until years later that I understood what had caused the engine to miss that day. Rainwater had entered the carburetor via the air intake, which is located in front of the plane. What Vanolli did was to close the air intake, which in turn provides the carburetor with hot air from the exhaust, a procedure called for during circumstances such as this, flying in precipitation, be it rain, snow or hail. The downside is that using hot air sacrifices engine performance, but it keeps the engine running without risk of quitting altogether.

We waited on the ground for a short while and when the downpour scattered and then stopped completely, Vanolli shouted, *"Vámonos!"*

He started and tested the engine for what seemed like a long time, and then we took off for Puerto Limon under a most radiant sun and with unlimited visibility. On this leg of the trip, Vanolli was back to his usual cheerful behavior. He seemed reassured and perhaps had reasons to be.

When we landed in Puerto Limon, Lacsa's DC-3 was

waiting for the delayed flight from Sixaola, and we were quickly ushered on board. My mother and I, at my insistence, sat in the first row, right aisle, so I could have an unobstructed view of the cockpit. It was my sought-after seat on the DC-3s. I remember vividly that the flight that day had a male flight attendant, which disappointed me enormously, since I was expecting the usual female Lacsa flight attendants who were always friendly and good-lookers, an attribute that even at that early age I appreciated. But not only that, to my dismay, the attendant, who must have been a budding pilot or enthusiast, stood right in the center of the cabin door, preventing me from seeing inside the cockpit. What rotten luck!

As power to those two Pratt & Whitney radial engines was applied, the airplane shuddered, broke its inertia and began to roll down the sand strip, gaining speed with every second. I felt the tail come off the ground and flutter slightly left and right. I could imagine the pilot working the tail rudder with the pedals to keep aligned with the narrow strip, his left hand on the control wheel and the right hand on the power levers. Right when I was expecting the airplane to lift off, I felt the plane swerve to the left. The attendant dashed and threw himself on the first unoccupied seat and quickly buckled his seatbelt and placed his feet against the bulkhead partition that separates the cockpit from the passenger compartment. The airplane gradually swung back and straightened, then lowered the tail while slowing down little by little. As we did a 180° turn and taxied back to the terminal, I realized that the left engine propeller was not turning. I had no idea what had happened. Once we parked, the pilot came out and informed us that the engine was damaged, and we would have to wait for another plane that would come from San Jose to pick us up. Lacsa bussed us to the Gran Hotel Caribe in town for lunch then back to the terminal. The replacement DC-3 arrived at dusk, seven hours later. It was a long wait, sitting on wooden benches in the tin roof terminal, but then I was used to that.

What had happened, and this again I was able to deduce years later, was a failure in the critical number one, left-side engine, and at the worst possible moment, at takeoff.[1-B]

Having experienced both those emergencies on the same day has stayed with me, especially the composure with which those pilots faced those uncertain situations. No panic under pressure. Years later, as a pilot I faced similar circumstances, and it makes me ponder if what happened that day somehow helped me prepare for what was to come.

Chapter 2
A World Apart

I was born and raised in Changuinola, a region isolated from the rest of the country so the arrival of aviation was a blessing. Whether it was in Copa or Lacsa DC-3s[2-A] or in Vanolli's single-engine Cessna, my earliest memory is traveling by air.

Before aviation arrived in the province, there were only two ways to get from Changuinola to David on the other side of the Cordillera.

The first option was to take a train from Changuinola to the port of Almirante, from there a passenger launch, the *Talamanca* or the *Changuinola*, to Bocas del Toro on Colon Island (Bocas). Once in Bocas, to continue by a coastal motor launch, either the *Stella Maris* or the *White Shadow* that sailed at dusk and traveled all night to arrive in the port of Colon at dawn the next day. Passengers disembarked in Colon and boarded the Panama Railroad Company train to Panama City. Since your final destination was David, you'd have to board yet another vessel to sail around the Azuero Peninsula all the way to Puerto Pedregal in Chiriqui province. That leg of the trip could take up to twenty-four hours. Once in Pedregal, a short train ride on the Chiriqui National Railroad (*Ferrocarril Nacional de Chiriquí*) took you to David. Fortunately, all this was long before I was born.

When the highway between Panama and David was inaugurated in 1931, it provided another option on that last leg, traveling by car. This took between twelve to twenty hours depending on the time of year. Both routes were exhausting to say the least.

The second option also required traveling by rail to Almirante to catch a motorized dugout *cayuco* to Chiriqui Grande, in Bocas del Toro province. There a trail known as La Cuesta began. The traveler either walked or rode a horse or mule over the mountains and ended up in Caldera, Chiriqui, a trip that could take two to three days. It should be noted that the distance between David and Changuinola, as the crow flies, is approximately 60 miles. At the beginning of the last century, my Kinkead maternal grandparents took this trip to Chiriqui Grande, Bocas del Toro, and back again years later with my mother as a newborn to Boquete, Chiriqui.

When commercial aviation did arrive in the province, it was like a blessing to the people of Changuinola and Bocas.

Once Copa and Lacsa started regular scheduled service to Changuinola from Panama City and San Jose, Costa Rica, respectively; progress took a foothold in the region. But for reasons that may have been technical or economic, first Lacsa and then Copa stopped providing that service to Changuinola. That void forced the passengers from Changuinola who wanted to travel to David or Panama City, to take the 4 a.m. train to Almirante, and from there a launch to Bocas, to catch one of the three weekly Copa flights to David or Panama. To go to San Jose, Costa Rica, passengers used the Sixaola connection with Vanolli. In those days punctuality and compliance were not the norm, so the waits could be extended a whole day or in some cases, until the next day. However, I don't remember feeling any inconvenience in that wait, because besides spending the night in my all time favorite Angelina Mama Peck's pension, the end result was, for me, the pleasure of flying in an airplane.

Exempt from these hardships were senior UFCo employees or high government officials, since both institutions had aircraft at their disposal.

Because of this reality, it is easy to understand why the people in that remote and isolated region, held airplanes and pilots in such high esteem.

Chapter 3
El Campo

The landing strip in Changuinola was at times used as a driving range by golfers, for baseball games and horse and bicycle races during Panama's Independence celebrations in November. El Campo, as it was commonly known, was located in Base Line, a community whose name came about when in 1909 the UFCo surveyed a baseline during the construction of a railroad that would link the banana plantations with the recently inaugurated port of Almirante.

Base Line was in those days the administrative center of the agricultural region. The post office, fire station, police station, the public school, and, most importantly, El Campo were all located there. The other important entities such as the hospital, rural dispensaries, commissaries, potable water and electricity installations, were spread strategically throughout the region and were managed by "the Company," as UFCo was referred to, and whose managerial headquarters were first based in Bocas, then in Guabito, near the Costa Rican border, then later transferred to Almirante and finally in Farm 8, in Changuinola. Although it hasn't been possible to ascertain exactly when the grounds were first used to land airplanes, the UFCo operated aircraft based in Honduras to shuttle its executives among the banana operations in Central America, Panama and Colombia since the early 1920s. So, it's likely that they were the first to use it. Records show that in 1921, CLC Bocas Division Manager Henry S. Blair arrived in Almirante from France Field, in Cristobal, on a floatplane. The UFCo inventory throughout the years, operated aircraft of various types including: a Fokker Universal, a Stearman C-2, a Lincoln Standard, a Beechcraft DS18, a Cessna 180, a Douglas DC-3, a Cessna 310, a Piper PA-31 Navajo, and finally a Beechcraft B-200, baptized as *Sweet Bocas*, which was based in Changuinola until the mid 1980s.

During the early years after initiating operations, El Campo was closed several times for one reason or another, but during those periods, the Company used a runway in Sixaola on the Costa Rican side to maintain a link between Changuinola and the rest of the banana operations inside and outside the country. In 1943, before I was born, the CLC transferred my father from the Puerto Armuelles Division in Chiriqui to the Bocas Division in Changuinola to oversee part of their recently begun abaca project,[3-A] so my parents and siblings traveled from Progreso, Chiriqui, to Sixaola on a Company plane. Although there are no records of who the pilot was, according to my father's narrations, it was Marcos A. Gelabert.[3-B]

During World War II, El Campo played an important role as a collection centre for the large number of agricultural workers from Central America recruited to work on the newly developed abaca project. Transporte Aéreo Centro Americano (Taca), a company started in Honduras in 1931, was contracted to transport Honduran, Salvadoran and Nicaraguan workers with their families to Changuinola. Persons who recall those days claim that Taca used both tri-motors and twin-engine airplanes, so it can be assumed with some certainty that they were Ford Tri-Motors and Lockheed Electras, since Taca operated both models during that period. If so, those flights would have been the first commercial flights to Changuinola.

Years later, in 1946, Taca included Changuinola as a stopover on its Albrook, Canal Zone, to San Jose, Costa Rica, route using DC-3s. Those DC-3s were the first recorded to use the Changuinola landing field. In 1947, Copa began regularly scheduled passenger and cargo operations connecting Changuinola with Panama and David for the first time. For a short period Lacsa linked San Jose, Costa Rica, with Changuinola with a stopover in Puerto Limon. Both companies operated DC-3s.

When Lacsa suspended flights connecting with Changuinola, Copa remained as the sole operator serving Changuinola with flights twice a week. Copa agent Saul Cholo Garcia would travel by train from Almirante to Changuinola on the days there were flights. To guarantee a space on any of those flights, the tickets had to be purchased in advance at his store in Almirante, which was inconvenient for those who didn't live there. Having access to a landline telephone and being counted among his reliable and trusted acquaintances was a great asset for obtaining a seat on the flight without investing a complete day traveling by train to buy a ticket prior to the flight.

Chapter 4
Airport Recollections

By the early 1950s, with the increase of aeronautical activity and to facilitate ground operations, the CLC took as its responsibility to maintain the grass runway and relinquished a building next to the runway that became the airport terminal for many years. The two-story wood house, the type assigned to the employees with the rank of foreman, had a zinc roof and wire-meshed windows. The first floor had planks nailed to the wall that served as benches for passengers, a counter with a chair and an antique weighing scale for both the cargo and passengers. There was a single bathroom in the back. Over the years, the building became inadequate since different airlines dispatched from there at the same time. A policeman, whose desk obstructed the entrance, kept track of the number of planes and passengers that arrived each day. After Copa's demise, the newly formed Rutas Aéreas Panameñas S.A. (Rapsa), the first company to resume scheduled flights to Changuinola, with their ten-passenger aircraft: two Boeings 247 and a Lockheed Electra, snatched the terminal for their exclusive use. Seats on the flight weren't guaranteed until the last minute before boarding. Elsie Howard, Rapsa's manager in Changuinola, became as important in the region as the CLC General Manager. Friendship, alliance and rank influenced who got on a flight or not.

For communications between the ground station and the airplanes in flight, Rapsa used a High Frequency (HF) radio. Elsie was in charge of judging the weather conditions for approaching flights. Her reports were basic but highly appreciated by the incoming pilots: "Rapsa, Rapsa, Changuinola here. It's raining but I can see the water tank. The wind is blowing from the south at about 10 knots," Elsie would report assertively. The water tank she referred to was the large 100-foot-high metal cylindrical tank coated with aluminum paint located on Runway 21's approach path a mile or so from the runway threshold. That was the determinant pilots used when approaching Changuinola with rain and low visibility: If you don't see the tank 30 seconds after crossing the coast line on a 210° heading, you missed the approach ... if you do see it, lower flaps to full and continue with the approach ... the runway is just ahead. I know this for a fact, it's one of the entries in my little red book, product of when years later I had to use that procedure as a pilot flying for Aero Perlas.

When Copa re-initiated scheduled service to Changuinola, their agent in Changuinola was Malcolm. He had to share the terminal with Elsie, who by seniority set the operating criteria. The competition between them was noticeable to everyone. As a passenger, one could expect consideration for getting a seat on a flight only if allied with one or the other. That's how staunch their rivalry was.

At the time, I had an after-school newspaper delivery business. Newspapers would arrive on the three weekly Copa flights from Panama City. My mode of delivery was by horseback. I made three cents per newspaper sold and because of the irregularity of the flights, I often picked up newspapers two to four days old, and although my clients accepted the backdated newspapers, at the end of the week when payment was due, they would claim that the newspapers were days old and simply would not pay.

Needless to say, the business was not lucrative, and I gave it up. But the up side of that activity was I had a legitimate excuse to go to the airport. The Stearman PT-17 crop-duster biplanes had just arrived to spray the bananas and they were a sight to see and hear. On Saturdays when there were no flights from Panama City, I would ride my horse to the airport to assist in any way possible in order to be in that environment of airplanes and pilots.

Arrivals and departures were events that nobody wanted to miss, so the airport was the place to be. Some were receiving or sending off relatives, others were there for the newspaper, but most were just looking for a distraction in a place that lacked it. As soon as the plane landed and the engines stopped, those on the ground surrounded the exit door or positioned themselves under the wing to receive and greet or simply to snoop out the arrivals. Being under the wing also offered protection from the radiant sun or the frequently drizzling rain. This informality at the airport developed into empathy between pilots with the *Changuinoleños*, to the point that locals had preferences regarding which company and even which pilots to travel with.

As a constant visitor to the airport, noteworthy occasions often occurred, such as when an Aerovías de Panamá S.A. (Avispa) DC-3 engine caught fire on start-up, causing the habitual on-lookers to stampede out of the area in Guinness-record time. Another time, a United States Air Force (USAF) C-47 came to transport several manatees captured in the Changuinola River lagoon to Gatun Lake in the Panama Canal for aquatic weed control, which turned into an all-day affair of improvised loading. Then there was the time that Captain Manuel Niño, with copilot Jorge Chial, had to belly-land a Rapsa

Boeing 247 because the landing gear failed to lower. Or when a Rapsa DC-3, commanded by James Red Grey[4-A] and Ezequiel Quielito Ledesma as copilot, got stuck in the mud and two farm tractors with dozens of volunteers pushing pulled it out. Or when Guillermo Billy Earle had to start one of his Copa DC-3 engines with a rope wound to the propeller hub and pulled by a pick-up truck because of a faulty starter motor. Or when a Rapsa C-47 freighter delivered the first private car brought to Changuinola, a Mini-Morris for Pucho Sanchez. Or when several steers broke away while being disembarked from an Internacional de Aviación (Inair) Curtiss-46 causing the Cuadrante neighborhood to resemble a local Pamplona running of the bulls. Or when the first jet airplane arrived during a demonstration flight, an Aeroflot Yak-40. Or when a Fuerza Aérea Panameña (FAP) C-47 on its last landing segment veered off the runway and nose crashed into the Atomizadora de Panamá (Atopan) hangar.

In retrospect, these events, though unanticipated and at times regrettable, were memorable; and only regulars to El Campo, like myself, were fortunate to witness them.

At the south end of the runway, in front of the former abaca plant, high voltage wiring approximately 50 feet high hung across the approach path. At the other end of the runway, to the north, there was a 50-foot ravine that at one time had been the channel of a tributary of the Changuinola River. While the direction and speed of the wind were the determinants of which of the runways to use, under calm wind conditions, the landings were usually to the southwest (Runway 21) and the takeoffs to the northeast (Runway 03), to avoid the high-tension wires. The Sanchez family lived in a house near the beginning of Runway 03, under the high tension cables, and the engine roar when planes passed a few feet above the roof prior to touching down was shocking, to put it mildly. But worse yet must have been watching the planes head directly toward the house at full speed on the takeoff run prior to lifting off.

The runway strip was originally grass and suitably long and wide for the airplanes of that time. When the planes were readying for takeoff with the tail towards the abaca plant, the group of kids and the ever-present dogs that never failed to be part of the action, would position themselves behind the airplane to challenge the strong airstream the engines produced at maximum power. Over the years and once the number of daily flights increased, the Civil Aeronautics Directorate of Panama (DAC) began to regulate the activities adjacent to the airport. The gathering of kids behind the airplane at takeoff was prohibited, but the dogs continued to be seen defying the slipstream until years later when the airport was modernized with an adequate terminal, parking lot, control tower, and a cyclone wire fence perimeter. From that moment, the field was never the same. It had lost its personality.

Left My first hero, Captain Francisco Vanolli Collado, Lacsa pilot and founder of Expreso Aéreo Costarricense, EXACO, in Limon, Costa Rica.

Right 1: Ford Tri-motor similar to those Taca used to transport Central American laborers to Changuinola in the 1940s.

Right 2: 1947 Cessna 170 registered to Servicio Aereo Vanolli S.A., circa 1950. Guapiles, Costa Rica, 2017.

Right 3: Aerial view of *Base Line* and the Changuinola landing strip. The channel can be seen at the head of Runway 21. On Runway 03 the buildings can be seen at the beginning of the runway. Map data ©2015 Google.

Below: Runway 21 at the edge of the ravine, Manuel Niño Airport, Changuinola, Panama.

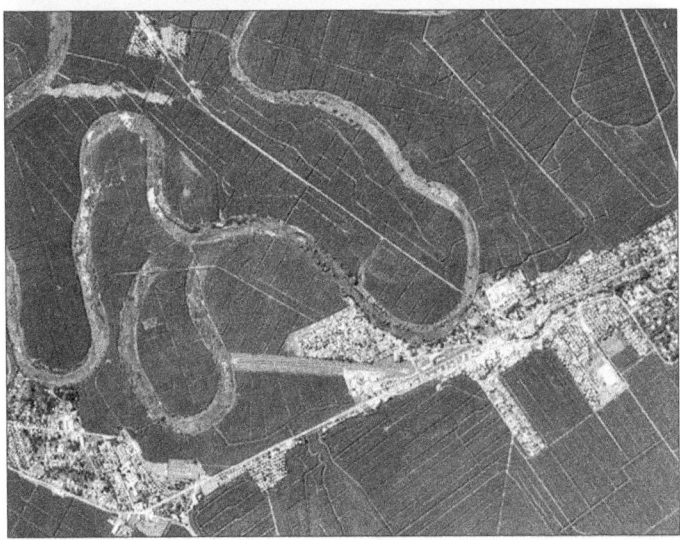

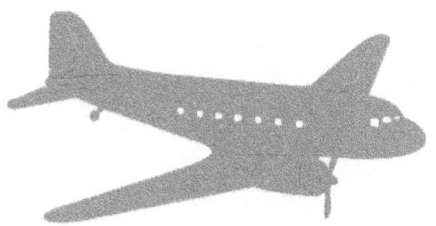

Part 2
The Beginning

5 Aeronautical Development
6 Aerial Spraying
7 Changuinola Loyalty

Chapter 5
Aeronautical Development

The strengthened and renewed investment in the banana industry in the late 50s and early 60s meant a boom in passengers and cargo to Changuinola. This motivated the formation of airlines dedicated to meet the demand with scheduled flights.

Although originally both Taca, Lacsa and Copa had started air service to Changuinola since 1946, and Avispa in 1956 for a brief period, it was Rapsa that first filled the vacuum left by Copa in the mid-1950s with regular flights from the Marcos A. Gelabert "Paitilla"[5-A] Airport in Panama City, in their Boeing B-247s and Lockheed Lodestar. Shortly after, Rapsa introduced the DC-3s and then a Martin 202. Copa renewed operations to Changuinola with its DC-3s, and years later with the Convair CV-340, Martin 404 and finally the HS Avro 748; Panacarga, a government-sponsored airline operated a Convair CV-580; Aerolíneas Urracá entered to compete with its DC-3s; Alas Chiricanas, who replaced Copa in 1980 on this route, initially operated DC-3s and later a Bandeirante EMB 110 and a DeHavilland Dash-7.

In the years of maximum operation, there were moments when airplanes crowded the airport's parking ramp. However, in 1984 this fast growing airborne activity was affected when the crude oil pipeline road from Charco Azul, Chiriqui, to Chiriqui Grande in Bocas del Toro was opened. A few years later, there was another marked decrease in air activity when the construction of the road section from Changuinola to Almirante was completed.

The final blow to the aeronautical boom at that time came with the completion of the section from Almirante to Chiriquí Grande in 2,000, connecting it with the Costa Rican border in Guabito. It never recovered.

After most of the aforementioned pioneering companies disappeared or stopped flying into Changuinola, Aero Perlas began providing service with DHC-6 Twin Otter, Beechcraft 200 and Shorts SD-360. Mapiex followed with the Fairchild Metroliner and Jetstream 31. But over time, these also disappeared. Today only Air Panama Regional provides itinerary service to Changuinola, renamed Capitan Manuel Niño International Airport, operating the Fokker 50. Of all the companies mentioned previously, only two are still active: Copa and Air Panama Regional.

Chapter 6
Aerial Spraying

In 1958, the CLC decided to rehabilitate the abandoned farms in Changuinola with another variety of banana resistant to the Panama disease that was decimating the Gros Michel banana plantations. Because of this significant increase in acres planted with the new variety, Lacatan, the CLC saw the need to look for more efficient ways to spray the farms against another fungus that was also threatening the plantations: Sigatoka. The traditional spraying practice up to that time consisted of a subterranean network of steel pipes with outlets for hoses and nozzles to spray the banana leaves.

This practice was slow and expensive. By 1959, the method of spraying fungicides radically changed. They contracted a British company, Fision Airworks Ltd. that operated under the license of Aeroquímica S.A. and used Hiller UH-12 helicopters to aerially spray a new low volume formula for Sigatoka fungus control. The pilots, as well as the mechanics, were British and Australian. In that sea of bananas that covered the Changuinola valley, *banderilleros* held flags on long bamboo poles to guide the pilots. At the end of the day the *banderilleros* ended up completely covered with chemical residue.

With the expansion of rehabilitated farms and the need for aerial sprayers with greater load capacity and coverage per flight, the Boeing Stearman PT-17 bi-plane, capable of heavier loads and higher performance, replaced the Hiller UH-12s. British, Belgians, and U.S. nationals, flew these fixed wing aircraft and among them Red Gray, who had originally been hired by the CLC to fly the North American T-6s used in a cloud seeding project in Puerto Armuelles. That cloud seeding project attempted to weaken the rainstorms that brought strong winds and caused "blow downs" that destroyed banana plantations. As for the banana spraying, a short time later the Snow S-2As, equipped with improved Microair spray nozzles replaced the Stearmans.

The Changuinola airport in Base Line was the base of operations for the sprayers in the Bocas Division. I was such a regular at the airport that I was allowed to help wash the aircraft and rinse the chemical hoppers. I felt privileged. It was impossible to get rid of the chemical odor that clung to my clothes, and my mother knew from the smell where I had been.

Emergency forced landings from mechanical failures were common, but not of great consequence, because they landed in a sea of bananas that cushioned the impact. If the damaged plane could not be fixed in the field and flown out after bulldozing a path in the middle of the bananas, it was disassembled and transported on a tractor-pulled cart to the airport. I witnessed several of these field repair operations. The pilots, who must have been mechanics as well, participated in all phases of the repair. Watching a plane fly after it was rebuilt was a sight to see. There was always a big celebration at the hangar when one of those rebuilt airplanes took to the air.

In those first days, there was only one fatal accident. Marc DeGuss, a Belgian pilot who had an engine failure on takeoff, crashed in the ravine at the end of the strip. A few weeks later a Colombian pilot arrived to replace him, and the operation continued as usual. The head of that operation was an Englishman, Jim Bernie, pilot and mechanic who was subsequently hired by Britten-Norman, a small aeronautical company on the Isle of Wight, England, as a test pilot. Britten-Norman was in the process of designing and manufacturing of a short takeoff and landing aircraft (STOL) to operate in marginal areas. This prototype, the Islander BN-2, became the workhorse of local companies based at Paitilla airport in Panama. The Islanders are still operating daily in the remote areas of San Blas and Darien, but now from the relocated Marcos A. Gelabert Airport in Albrook.

With the increase of banana spraying activity, Aeroquímica S.A. began to hire Panamanian technical personnel. The first mechanics hired for operations in Changuinola were Alberto Lewis, Ruben Lance McQueen, Isaac Martinez, Ernesto Ruth, Eduardo Noble Hansell and Eduardo Bali Herrera, all from Bocas. Manuel Niño, who had flown in Rapsa since its inception, was the first Panamanian spray pilot hired. Unfortunately, he died in an accident in October 1960 while flying a Snow S-2A. At the time, the banana company had installed a cable system that crisscrossed the farms to transport suspended bunches of fruit from the farm to the packing plant. These steel cables, half an inch in diameter, became a significant risk for the pilots who had to forcibly land while spraying the banana fields.

In 1961, Aero Química S.A. became Atomizadora de Panamá (Atopan) with a fleet of sixteen planes operated in Changinola and Puerto Armuelles. In 1973, the Rockwell Thrush Commander S-2R replaced the S-2A. The guidance system for the pilots was redesigned and lighter aluminum tubes with pulleys to raise and lower the flags replaced the original bamboo poles, but the *banderillero* was still exposed to sprayed chemicals.

In 1981, Atopan's Tam Syme proposed implementing in Changuinola an innovative technique that eliminated the need for *banderilleros*. Called the Flying Flagman, it used towers equipped with transmitters at both ends of the plantations to guide the pilots electronically by using a transponder on the airplane. Once the Flying Flagman was implemented, *banderilleros* were no longer required, and were relocated to other agricultural jobs.

By 1982, the first Turbo Thrush S-2RT made its appearance in both the Bocas and Puerto Armuelles divisions. Although the Flying Flagman was innovative at the time, it was nothing compared to the methodology in use today. The Global Positioning System (GPS) works by satellite and is used in aerial application operations to guide the spray pilots worldwide.

In 2014, the Brazilian company Cutrale-Safra acquired Chiquita Brands International, including CLC that administered the Changuinola banana operations. Today, extensive banana operations exist only in the Caribbean region, because in 2003 the United Brands banana cultivation in Chiriqui on the Pacific side transferred to a workers' cooperative, COOSEMUPAR. The cooperative ran operations until 2008 when it declared bankruptcy.

Atopan continues to spray bananas in Changuinola and is associated with Colonos Agropecuaria S.A, a Costa Rican company. The operations are conducted with the Ayres Thrush and Air Tractor aircraft with PT-6 turbines. The need to control Sigatoka has not changed, and the constant adjustment of doses, elements, emulsions, frequencies and types of chemicals has helped to maintain a thriving banana industry in Bocas del Toro.

Chapter 7
Changuinola Loyalty

The loyalty of the *Changuinoleños* towards Rapsa was impressive since it was the company that resumed air service after Copa and Lacsa had departed and Avispa had disappeared. From the start, Rapsa was very accommodating with its passengers: If a flight was cancelled one day, the next day they would assure travel to all the passengers that had been left, or if there were more passengers for the number of seats, an additional flight was programmed no matter the time of day.

Even though some time later Copa renewed its scheduled service to Changuinola with its DC-3s, the *Changuinoleños* favored traveling with Rapsa unless there was no space available. Rapsa eventually had a DC-3 based in David that allowed it to make an early morning flight over the Cordillera before the Copa flight from Panama, capturing the day's quota of passengers. Rapsa also scheduled an afternoon Cordillera crossing to Changuinola, a previously unknown advantage for both David and Changuinola merchants. With time, Copa opted for the same set-up and had a plane based in David. It was a sight to see two DC-3 aircraft approaching Changuinola vying to land first. Rapsa, always in competition with Copa, reached an agreement with independent banana producers so that their workers could buy and reserve seats directly from the farm offices and thus save the hassle and the cost of going to the airport days before to buy their tickets in order to guarantee their seat in the plane. With the land transportation service as inefficient as it was, this was a valued option.

Part of the mystique that Rapsa had with the locals was the pilot-passenger relationship. A living example in my memory was on a flight to Panama City on a Rapsa DC-3. I was standing in my usual spot between the pilots in the cockpit, when after the takeoff and initiating climb, I realized that I had left my passport, travel tickets to the US, and traveler's checks to pay for a semester in boarding school in the airport terminal. When I informed Coco Garzon, the captain of that flight, of my plight, he immediately banked the airplane back towards the runway and landed. Before the surprised look of the many who were still at the airport, I jumped off the plane without waiting for the stairs, ran to where my parents were standing still holding the yellow folder containing the documents, grabbed it and jumped back on the plane, all this time with the engines running. The flight attendant closed the door, and we were back in the air in minutes, this time non-stop, straight to Panama City. I'm certain that this operation could not take place on a commercial flight today.

Since the CLC had benefited from the renewal of the air transport service in Changuinola, one can also understand its preference of Rapsa over Copa. In turn, CLC favored Rapsa as their sole courier, as well as the choice airline to transport staff on official and social trips such as managerial meetings and sports activities in Puerto Armuelles, Puerto Limon and Golfito, Costa Rica.

On one occasion, consistent with its expansion program, the CLC was venturing into the Asian market, specifically Japan, so it hired Rapsa's Boeing 247 to transport a load of bananas to Panama City, where they would be shipped on a refrigerated ship to Japan. The flight was expected to arrive at Changuinola at 2 p.m. to pick up the cargo of bananas. The CLC's management staff, local authorities and dozens of onlookers, including my brother Pillo and me, had been there since early afternoon. It was going to be an event worthy of a celebration: The first shipment of bananas in corrugated cardboard boxes by air.

Hours went by and nothing. By late afternoon, the CLC brass and local authorities began to leave in their respective cars. Only a few, who were convinced that the flight would arrive, stayed on. The sky had already turned dark when we heard a roar of engines flying over the field. It was Rapsa's Boeing 247!

Those who had cars had already left, and it took some time to locate and get them to return. Their headlights were needed to light the runway. Once that was achieved, the Boeing 247 landed without delay. Red Gray was the captain, Ñemo Chiari the copilot, accompanied by a young woman. By this time, the airport was full of on-lookers from the Cuadrante, a CLC workers' housing compound adjacent to the runway. They had heard the plane flying overhead and hurried to the runway. It was an uncommon event. Darkness engulfed the area once the car lights were extinguished. The Boeing had to take on fuel for the return flight so it wasn't until after 8 p.m. when they finally took off with the first shipment of boxed bananas to Asia. Again, Rapsa had fully complied with its loyal followers. I can still see the flames spitting from the exhaust of the Boeing 247's radial engines as it climbed eastward.

I came to recognize by name and fly as a passenger with most of the captains that flew the DC-3 and the Curtiss C-46 that operated sporadically in those days. Many have already passed to another life, such as Captains Miguel Aristides Ñopo DePuy, Carlos Cowes, Manuel Amador Pitti, Ricardo Ledesma, Bolita Castro, James Red Gray, Jose Coco Garzon,

Jose Pepe Chavarria, Ignacio Chacho Inchausti, Hermes Carrizo, Jorge Chial, Richard Prescott, Venancio Mendez, Ezequiel Quielito Ledesma, Paul Perez, and Constantino Tinito Romero.

Something worthy of mention was the commotion at Changuinola airport when the first Panamanian, Miguel Aristides DePuy, arrived as captain of a DC-3. Before that, all the captains were US citizens since Copa, as a Pan American Airways subsidiary, had its own supply of pilots at the beginning. Little by little, after that event, Panamanian copilots were promoted to occupy the coveted left seat. The second was the charismatic Captain Carlos Cowes.

Already in my teens, whenever I had to travel with one of the known pilots, my usual position was in the cockpit, to the extent that I knew from memory the cockpit procedures before, during and after a DC-3 flight. I think that experience sealed my childhood longing to fly.

In these wanderings as an observer in the cockpit, I happened to be present during several critical situations that I feel were of great value for the future: An engine failure crossing the Cordillera and another coming out of Tocumen. The engine-out emergency procedures executed were timely and effective. I feel privileged to have witnessed those emergencies first-hand inside the cockpit because the norm is that flight emergency training is simulated. Those two were real.

At the beginning of the 70s, Captain Amador Pitti, Rapsa's Chief of Operations, arranged for a Russian 27-passenger Yak-40 to fly to Changuinola for demonstration as a possible acquisition of the company. The Yak spent several days crossing the Cordillera back and forth between David and Changuinola. The passengers were noticeably skeptical as they boarded an airplane that didn't have propellers, but I doubt that this was the reason why Rapsa desisted from acquiring it. Rather I think it was the purchase price, its operational cost, and its lack of versatility as a freighter. The latter was an important deliberation considering the type of cargo that was prevalent in the region. The company, wisely I think, decided not to replace the venerable DC-3.

Had I known in March of 1972, while flying in a chartered freighter to transfer our family belongings from Changuinola to Panama City, that it would be the last time I'd travel in a Rapsa DC-3, I would have given greater importance to that flight. The captain was Quielito Ledesma and Ernesto Ponce was his copilot. I always appreciated Ernesto's gesture of allowing me to occupy his copilot's seat that day, although on second thought, I suspect that it was more his desire to go and settle in one of the sofas that was part of the cargo, than to share his portion of the flying time.

The following year, in 1973, Rapsa stopped flying its last two DC-3s, and with that, a legacy that deeply marked the province of Bocas del Toro, especially Changuinola and me in particular, ended.

Above: Copa HP-86 on final, Runway 03, Changuinola, over the Sanchez family house. Note the electric cables.

Below: Captain Quielito Ledesma boarding Rapsa's DC-3. Julita Gonzalez greeting the passengers at the top of the stairs.

Above: Ibu on the cargo flight from Changuinola - Tocumen. Rapsa DC-3, 1972.

Above 1: Peak hours at the Changuinola airport ramp.

Above 2: Copa HP-87. Typical Changuinola airport scene during the 1950s and 60s.

Above 3: Father John Kennedy boarding Copa HP-86 in Changuinola.

Above 1: Boeing 247 similar to the ones operated by Rapsa.

Above 2: Rapsa DC-3. Tocumen Airport, Panama.

Above 3: Panamanian Air Force DC-3. Tocumen, Panama.

Above: Spraying bananas in Changuinola, Bocas del Toro, Panama.

Above: Elsie Howard (right) and her secretary Chica Barrera in the Rapsa office, Changuinola.

Part 3
Initiation

8 The Bug Bites
9 Pheromones Aloft
10 Formal Instruction

Chapter 8
The Bug Bites

Despite that there was considerable air activity in Changuinola in the 60s, there were no flying clubs or schools like there were in Santiago, David and Panama City, mainly because the flights didn't originate or end in Changuinola. Passenger and cargo operations to and from Changuinola were based in Panama City and David, with the exception of the foreign crop dusting companies that brought their own pilots, since there were no local crop dusting pilots. The few Bocas pilots in those days, like Celso Gallimore and Efrain Pin Herrera, had left the province to get flight training elsewhere. The opposite occurred in Santiago, David and Paitilla in Panama City, which produced dozens of pilots that filled the few vacancies available.

In 1968, I had just graduated from a US university as an agricultural engineer, a commitment I had made with my parents, and was managing the family banana business, Finca Terronal in Changuinola. However, I was eager to start flying at the first opportunity.

Aulio Hernandez, who had flown Copa's DC-3s and now flew the CLC's Piper Navajo, along with other local enthusiasts, had formed a flying club in Almirante. The club purchased two Cessnas, a 150 and a 172 and negotiated with the CLC the use of a tract of land for a runway strip. The heavy shrubs were cleared and bulldozed into a landing strip minutes away from the Almirante town site.

It's important to realize that to get to Almirante from Changuinola took an hour ride by train, and there was only one option either way: the 7 a.m. train to Almirante and the 4 p.m. train back to Changuinola. To get away from the farm for a whole day to take flying lessons was unjustifiable, besides there was no guarantee of getting in any flight time at all. The perennial problem of availability of the airplanes and instructors was a strong factor to consider. It always seemed like either the plane was down for maintenance or another student had it, or the weather was bad for flying or the instructor wasn't available. After sacrificing four days in two weeks and having achieved a total of three hours of flight training, I was so frustrated that I gave up completely.

One morning, while at the farm I got a phone call from the Changuinola airport informing me that someone with an airplane wanted to talk to me. I had no idea who it could be. Someone had told Reinaldo Giraud from Santiago de Veraguas that I wanted to buy a plane, and he had come to interest me in his plane: a 1947, 90-horsepower Aeronca Champion. It was a fabric-covered airplane, not like the more modern aluminum ones. The aircraft was equipped with basic instrumentation: compass, airspeed, altimeter, oil temperature and pressure and RPM. That was it. It had a pull starter motor but no other electrical components, so there were no communication or navigational radios, or instrument, cockpit or landing lights. Neither did it have wing flaps, and the brakes were the antique heel type, not the more modern toe brakes. It had a stick protruding from the middle of the floor in front of each of the front and back seats instead of a wheel yoke. In short, no whistles and bells. It was an airplane designed back in the 1940s to teach flying. I remember thinking that if he had crossed the Cordillera from Santiago that morning, it must be a reliable plane. The moment I entered the tight cabin, I was captivated not only by the aura of it all, but also by the smell of gasoline and oil that only old airplanes have. After a 20-minute demonstration flight, I was hooked and agreed to buy it on the spot for USD $2,100.00 cash. That same day I obtained a personal loan to buy the Aeronca in the Cooperativa Bananera de la Vertiente Atlántica (COBAVA). I took her up that very afternoon, my first flight at the controls to fly from Changuinola to Bocas where there was a Notary Public to document the sale. Once that was done, Reinaldo shook my hand and handed me the keys to the Aeronca.

"Here you go. Enjoy it. I'm staying on the island to catch the morning Rapsa flight to David."

"Hold on, hold on," I said, "I've never flown by myself before."

"What do you mean? You've never flown without an instructor? But hey, that's not a problem. I'll fly back with you to the farm strip, and I'll check you en route. This plane is very easy to fly. It flies at 35, cruises at 80 and stalls at 35. That's all you have to know."

Probably driven by the enthusiasm of owning an airplane, I convinced myself it would be a piece of cake to learn to fly this airplane. I flew the Aeronca back to the farm, practicing stalls and power changes. Reinaldo coached me down all the way to the landing and once out of the plane, reiterated, "Remember: 35, 80, 35."

My previous few hours of instruction in the Cessna 150, which was a tricycle airplane with a nose steering wheel, hadn't prepared me for what was coming. The Aeronca was a conventional gear aircraft, making it more difficult to maneuver on the ground. However, once achieved, it's a rewarding challenge, but that knowledge came later, much later.[8-A]

Luis Flores, our neighbor who owned a Cessna 180 taildragger, offered to check me out in the Aeronca. For one reason or another, that never materialized. But Lucho, his son and my contemporary who was quite advanced in his flying at Aulio's flight school in Almirante, offered to teach me however much or little he knew. We flew together for almost three hours, but again, he made the take-offs and landings, since he had had some practice flying with his father in the 180. All that was fine, but I wasn't getting any closer to flying my plane by myself.

Tam Syme, who had been an instructor pilot in the British Royal Air Force (RAF), and who was now flying for Atopan, had been giving me ground school on navigation, aerodynamics, meteorology and power plant in the Atopan hangar after work. When I told him of my predicament, he offered to give me first hand practical lessons in the Aeronca. The plan was for him to give me a few minutes of flight instruction from the farm strip on the days he was spraying bananas in the area. Usually he finished flying by 7 a.m. It was a great arrangement and I felt fulfilled. I was finally on the road to flying my airplane by myself.

At 6:30 the next morning I was waiting for him ready for my first real instruction in a taildragger. He hopped out of the Thrush Commander he was flying, leaving the motor running and jumped in the back seat of the Aeronca to give me the basics of flying an airplane. He used the first few minutes of that 20-minute flight to familiarize himself with the plane. Then he demonstrated slow flight, steep turns and stalls, with and without power. Before climbing back to his Thrush Commander, he advised I practice taxiing the plane, since a taildragger pilot must learn to master these squirrely aircraft with the wheel on the tail. The secret was practice, practice and more practice, taxiing. During the next few days I'd get up before dawn and before starting my chores at the farm, I'd practice taxiing up and down the runway, then again at noon after lunch, and at dusk before dark. I taxied at different speeds until I felt in control, although, not without a couple of scares when I veered off the centerline of that narrow asphalt runway. Lucky for me there were no witnesses to how troublesome it was for me to get a handle on that little airplane. Twice a week for a couple of weeks, in the few minutes available, I practiced takeoffs and landings with Tam, until one morning he told me I was ready to fly Solo.

"What about the eight regulatory hours of instruction to qualify for Solo?" I asked. Actually I already had a total of about fifteen hours of flight time, although only about five of official instruction, but he didn't need to know that small detail.

"Just go fly the airplane!" he said and then he got in his Thrush and took-off to Atopan's home base at the Changuinola airport.

I looked at the Aeronca, then took three deep breaths and asked myself if it wasn't now, then when? I got in the plane, strapped in, started the engine and taxied to the end of the runway. Let's do it! Accelerate slowly. Roll in a straight line down the center; raise the tail with forward stick and wait for the correct speed. What was is it, 35 or 40? No, 35; ease stick back, softly. That's it. Let her climb by herself. There, we're flying. Calm down; take a deep breath. Slowly, level the plane. Softly. What's the speed, 80? I'm only going 70. What's wrong, why so slow? Are we stalling? Add power. Lower the nose; not so much, we're still low. How high are we? 400 feet. Let's go up a little bit more, to 800 feet. Turn left. Ball in the center, that's right.[8-B] What's the flight pattern height, 500 feet? I'm high, keep going around and drop to 500 feet. We're going too fast; reduce power. Not so much, that's it. Line up with the runway and reduce power to approach at 60, no, 50. That's right; just stay calm. We're high; lower the nose, not so much. Reduce power, cut it back to idle; we're coming in high. We're going to overshoot. Slow it down, slowly. We're over the runway. Why aren't we touching down? We're floating, what do I do, pull the stick farther back to stall it or give it power and go around or ... Pum, Pum, Pum. Hey! We landed and the plane is not broken! Wait; wait, now here comes the tricky part. Keep it in a straight line, be careful, don't ground loop. That's it. Go easy on the brakes. There you go. I made it! Piece of cake! Whew!

That first Solo flight wasn't ceremonious at all, but not having the external pressures on an occasion like this was advantageous. There was no instructor scrutinizing me; there were no other pilots waiting to drench me in oil or tear my shirttail off; nor were the habitual airport regulars, or anything of the sort waiting to see a novice pilot mess-up. I did it in full privacy on an isolated farm runway, on a cool morning, with little wind. However, on the down side, nobody was around to celebrate the great feat. My first and only Solo flight! There would never be another first solo flight ever again. That first solo flight gives a sense of skill, of mastery over space and time and life itself. A remarkable one-time experience indeed.

At 8 a.m. on August 1, 1969, after that somewhat unconventional start to aviation, I decided to fly every day possible. I did it early in the morning and in the twilight, my favorite hour. Little by little I came to recognize shadows and clearings as I approached to land shortly after sunset. Every day I extended my flight radius; following the railway line as a guide to Guabito and Almirante and to Bocas Island using the marine buoys as orientation. I felt confident, to the extent that I even extended my flights to land right as darkness fell, until the day arrived when I put an abrupt stop to all that.

I had flown to the port of Almirante to witness a banana shipment, and in passing, to visit a recently arrived American School teacher, who had captured my eye. I must have lost track of time because it was beginning to get dark as I rode to the airport in Almirante's only taxi at the time. However, since I had practiced flying at dusk, I felt confident and decided to leave anyway. What I didn't take into consideration was that between Almirante and Changuinola there was nothing to help me navigate other than the railroad that cut through a dense canopy of jungle, and at night, not even that was visible. Halfway there, absolute darkness suddenly surrounded me. I could see nothing outside the cabin, neither front nor back, or to the sides, or inside the cockpit. Shit! What have I gotten myself into now?

I couldn't return to Almirante, an unfamiliar runway was not an option. I had to keep going, at least Changuinola was familiar, my back yard. The Aeronca had a compass, but I couldn't see it because of the darkness. Neither was the railroad visible. Maintaining the last heading was the only way out. So I did. I pressed the stick with both my knees and anchored my feet on the pedals. I didn't even dare blink an eye. It was like flying blindfolded, nothing but blackness. At least the engine kept purring on, oblivious to my problem. After a while, which seemed like hours, I saw some lights ahead in the distance. I presumed that it had to be Farm 4, and there beyond the Changuinola River bridge. I never saw the bridge in the darkness, but I did identify the lights of El Empalme and the houses located on both sides of the railroad line. I knew they would take me to the Changuinola airport, but the airport had no lights, so I was still not out of the mess I had gotten myself into. The Changuinola runway is oriented northeast to southwest, but without being able to read the compass, it was useless knowledge. The runway was covered with black asphalt, so in the dark it was of no help to me. I kept my approach high on purpose, with the high-tension electrical cable in mind. I knew that the houses bordering the Cuadrante were skewed to the runway orientation, so I aimed the Aeronca's nose slightly to the right of the line of lights. With no depth perception, I just let the airplane descend slowly until all three wheels touched ground. That was it; the plane hopped once and then settled down and stopped. There was nobody around to witness. I think nobody even heard the engine, because in those days the Costa Rican TV signal could be tuned-in and that paralyzed the whole community at night; everyone was watching *Chucho el roto*, a popular Mexican novel. After securing the airplane, I borrowed a phone from *don* Juan Upegui, a Colombian who ran the Commissary next to the airport, and called the farm. Pedro Villareal, our farm driver and mechanic, arrived shortly and helped me to push the Aeronca to a safe place off the runway. On the way home I made him swear to secrecy what had just transpired. After the initial shock and after analyzing what had happened, my first night flight, I decided: Never again. I recognized then that it was a good lesson, and after so many years, I still vividly remember that fright. That was the first note in my little red book under the "Never Again" category.

For the next three months I flew at every possible moment and took as many people who dared accompany me, including my parents. My first passenger was my father. And of course, the Almirante teacher was my most frequent passenger, without imagining that one day she would become my wife.

It wasn't until one day after landing in Changuinola that Alvaro Ricoy, who had been my initial instructor at the Almirante Aero club and who was now flying in Copa's DC-3s, pulled me aside and demanded to know what I was doing flying alone without a valid instructor's approval.

"Well," I said, "let's go up and check me out."

So we did. He got in the back seat and we flew about ten minutes demonstrating a series of maneuvers including an unsuspected emergency, where he pulled back the engine power just before taking off. I was able to recover and skillfully settle the plane back down again. I had practiced that maneuver innumerable times because Tam had drilled it in me that the most critical moment of a flight was to lose power on take-off. Once we landed, he let me know in no uncertain terms that although I knew how to fly the plane, if I didn't apply for a student's permit from DAC in Panama City, and get a medical certificate, and pass a private pilot ground school, and take flying lessons from a certified instructor, he would report me to the authorities. *Ras!*

Now what? I couldn't take leave from the numerous farm responsibilities for so long a time to go to Panama City to meet all these requirements. Again I was at a crossroads. A few days later I happened to receive a notification from the British embassy in Panama that I had been selected for a two-year Post Graduate scholarship in Hydrology in Great Britain. My long awaited recently initiated aviation career had to be put on hold for the second time. It was November 1969.

Chapter 9
Pheromones Aloft

In 1971, after the 1969 and 1970 floods that decimated a large portion of the banana plantations in the Bocas del Toro province, a prolonged drought hit the rest of the country, especially the central provinces. Agriculture and livestock suffered from lack of water; cattle died and without rain, rice, corn, beans and sorghum crops couldn't be sown. Not so in Bocas del Toro. Because there is no such thing as a dry season there, the pastures were green all year round.

Taking advantage of the circumstances, Ganadera Bocas negotiated the purchase of live cattle in the Cocle region to increase its herd of cattle in the San San pastures in Guabito. Arrangements were made with Inair, an air cargo outfit, to transport the cattle from the Rio Hato airport on the Pacific coast directly to Changuinola.

I had recently returned to Changuinola after my two-year absence in the United Kingdom, and I was at the airport with Ramon Mon Arauz, who managed Ganadera Bocas for *don* Mario Guardia, the day the first flight arrived with fifteen skinny young bulls. The plane was a Curtiss Commando C-46, especially configured for transporting livestock. The pilot, Captain Richard Prescott, was fuming over the lack of coordination in the Rio Hato operation. He complained that they wouldn't be able to transport all the cattle programmed for that day, and that someone should be in Rio Hato to direct the operations there like the one here in Changuinola. Mon, who didn't like riding in planes much less a freighter like this one, asked if I would take over running the Rio Hato loading operation.

"Sure, I'll go!" I replied instantly. I hadn't flown since I got back and was feeling frustrated. While away, I had sold my Aeronca to Aulio Hernandez for the Almirante Aeroclub and was left without a plane.

Before we boarded the C-46, I asked for a helper and was assigned a Ganadera Bocas cowboy, Chiricano, (as one hailing from the Chiriqui province) who had never been close to a plane in his life, much less flown in one. This particular C-46 smelled strongly of urine and cattle pooh, and inside the cargo cabin even more so. Sawdust covered the plywood floor, so it wasn't practical to sweep or wash it while the operation was on going. The corrals were made of removable aluminum tubing that could be assembled into pens of different sizes. The crew consisted of Captain Prescott and copilot Alexis DePuy. It was the first time I had met them. Much later I learned that Captain Prescott had flown the C-46s during World War II crossing the Hump, the Himalayan range, to transport war material from Assam, India, to Chinese troops who were resisting the invading Japanese army in Kunming, China. During that India-Burma-China campaign, the Curtiss Commando demonstrated its sturdiness and was recognized as an ideal airplane for this type of operation. I guess both Captain Prescott and this C-46 were in their environment that day. Since there were no seats other than for the flying crew and the observer, Chiricano stood behind me in the observer's seat in the ample cockpit. While the copilot flew a direct southeast route to Rio Hato crossing the mountain range at 9,500 feet in severe turbulence typical for that time of year, Captain Prescott explained the situation. His Spanish pronunciation was difficult to decipher, but he made himself understood. He detailed his frustration with the lack of organization during the cattle loading at Rio Hato.

As soon as we landed and the doors were opened, I understood instantly why Captain Prescott was so upset. A hoard of cattle trucks started vying to get to the front of the line to load their cargo. I climbed on the roof of one of the trucks and shouted to let them know that it was important to load the plane according to the weight of the cattle, not by who was first in line. But their desire to load their cattle and guarantee the sale overcame reason. They were afraid lo lose the opportunity to sell their herd. We suspended the operation until we could come up with an acceptable methodology for the sellers, the buyer and the carrier, in this case Inair. Since most of the cattle were unbranded, I suggested spot painting their rumps with different color paint. So we sent a taxi to buy five one-gallon cans of different color paints, and we explained to the owners that although the cattle would be mixed on the flights, the colors would identify which were theirs. The proposal was reluctantly accepted and the loading began, selecting the cattle by estimated weight. That sped up the operations and we were able to make three trips without mishap.

It was important to load the aircraft according to the weight of the cattle because of the aircraft's weight and balance restrictions. The center of gravity (C.G.) of every aircraft is determined by the weight of the load (pounds) and balance (location). If the C.G. is off balance, it is neither safe nor legal to fly. Since we didn't have a weighing scale, having brought Chiricano along proved to be a great advantage. He deftly looked over each animal and estimated its weight. We had no other option but to trust his "eyeballing" technique.

We had decided to leave a big, heavy Brahman stud bull that weighed about a ton for the last trip since he was visibly upset and would cause us trouble if he didn't calm down. He had been confined in a truck in the sun without water all day. The rationale was that by the afternoon the north winds would have subsided and there wouldn't be as much turbulence, which could alter our rebellious passenger even more. While crossing the mountain range on our trip back to pick up our last load, we noticed that the strong winds and the turbulence still persisted. Not a good sign.

Captain Prescott decided that it was best to fly straight north, cross the mountain range at its lowest and narrowest point, reach the Caribbean coast and then turn west until we reached Changuinola. That way we avoided being exposed to turbulence for too long, and we wouldn't have to fly so high. This route would take longer than the forty-five minutes on our earlier direct flights. It was getting late so we would have to speed up the loading before it got too dark.

Getting that Brahman bull inside the airplane was a major undertaking. He kicked, tried goring, he drooled through his mouth and nose. He definitely didn't want to board the Curtiss at all. He was pushed by the haunches, pulled by the jaws and given electric shocks with a prodding rod. Nothing worked. He just would not budge. Once again Chiricano saved the situation by grabbing his tail and biting it. That did it. The Brahma jumped and bellowed while he dashed to the corral in front of the plane, behind the cockpit. Once in the corral he became enraged again. He kicked and rammed his horns through the aluminum railings, splitting the wooden boards that protected the inside of the fuselage. There was no way we could take off with a situation like that. Why didn't we think to bring the Ganadera Bocas veterinarian who was in Changuinola? He could have given the bull a tranquilizer, but then again, hindsight is 20/20.

Then Chiricano approached me and said, "*Jefe*, let's throw some heifers on the plane to accompany the beast. Being in their company just might calm him down."

Damn, I said to myself, if this cowboy has already proven to possess instinctive know-how, why not now? Right away we gave the order to load up some heifers. We quickly assembled a second corral next to where the bull was and selected four skinny heifers. The heifers were quiet so there was no need to tie them up. The bull watched the goings-on with a sideways glance, but he did seem calmer.

"Ready. Let's go. Move the truck. We're closing the doors." I felt relieved that at last we were taking off. It had been a long day, and it was not over yet.

As soon as we took off, we could see to the west that the sun was sinking toward the horizon. The atmosphere inside the cockpit felt heavy, but in reality it was the exhaustion of an arduous day and the heat that gave no respite. Both crewmembers had taken off their shirts and were in sweat-stained T-shirts. The smell of urine and cattle dung was even stronger than when we started the job in the morning.

I leaned forward in my observer's seat and asked Captain Prescott, "Captain, you're aware that in Changuinola there are no runway lights, right?"

"Don't worry. We're following the sun," was his immediate response. Well, yes, I rationalized, once we cross the mountain range we will be turning towards the west, towards the sun, following it. All's good.

The ascent was slow with the intention of causing the least disturbance to our illustrious passenger. Once we reached 4,500 feet, we crossed a low saddle in the mountain range, and turned left towards Changuinola. Looking to the left and back we could see Rio de Jesus, Veraguas, on the Caribbean coast. All's good.

Once we were established on a westerly course with Punta Valiente in sight, we felt a huge shudder and the airplane's nose pitched up. We all knew instantly that what had happened was caused by the bull. Captain Prescott immediately applied down pressure to the yoke and simultaneously readjusted the elevator trim to stabilize the aircraft.

"Check it out!" he says without turning to look at anyone in particular. I rapidly unbuckle my seat belt and when I enter the cargo compartment, I see the bull with the front half of his body swinging in the upper tube of the corral that separates him from the corral with the heifers. He is facing the back of the fuselage and keeps trying to get into the heifer's corral. Chiricano is shouting at the bull and hitting him in the head with a rope to dissuade him.

"Hold it, hold it. You're making things worse. It's infuriating him even more. Leave him alone," I shout and go back to the cabin to inform Captain Prescott that the bull is half inside the heifer pen. We both know that if he were to escape from the second corral, he'd be loose in the rear most section of the plane, and to have a ton or so moving freely around would make it impossible to control the plane.

The tension in the cabin is palpable. The three of us know the danger of an unbalanced airplane. Suddenly the door opens and Chiricano exclaims, "*Jefe, Jefe*, the bull just jumped into the heifers' corral!"

Mierda! Now he's only a hop away from breaking free. Damn it!

"No, no. I don't think so. He'll be quiet now that he's accompanied with his heifers. You'll see," Chiricano assures us.

All this time, Prescott is attentive to the conversation and snaps, "Shit!"

The four of us remain silent in the cockpit, maybe convinced that the problem will just go away. The plane is flying normally with no perceived changes in its center of gravity. Now all that's left is to hope that the bull doesn't get any romantic ideas.

With adrenaline levels almost back to normal, I suddenly realize that it's gotten dark. It's 6:30 p.m. and you can see the lights of Bocas Town, and in the distance those of Almirante, and even of Changuinola. The copilot tries in vain to communicate first with the Bocas tower and then with Changuinola. Both close at 6 p.m.

Already on descent and passing Almirante to our left, I venture to advise Captain Prescott, "Look, Captain, I recommend you approach runway 03 since a line of houses more or less line up with the runway at that end and help you get oriented. But be advised that there's a high voltage cable crossing the beginning of the runway about 40 to 50 feet high."

All this time I was recalling a similar situation that I had with the Aeronca years before, with the striking differences: that night it had been dark, this one is moonlit; the Aeronca didn't have landing lights, this C-46 does; and also, more importantly, that night I had maybe 25 hours of flight experience, Captain Prescott must have tens of thousands of hours of experience. Big difference.

"Gear down, quarter flaps, easy does it, half flaps, easy, easy. Full flaps, easy does it, keep the tail low, slow it down, easy, easy," the captain reminded himself, as if he were alone in the cockpit. We were already aligned with the runway because we could see the shadow of the black asphalt against the lighter grass up ahead and the lights of the Cuadrante houses that appeared skewed to our heading. All's good.

Suddenly, POW! An explosion-like noise overtook us, and the Cuadrante lights that had guided us to line up with the runway went out. Captain Prescott didn't even flinch, he kept repeating: "Easy does it, keep the tail low, slow it down, easy, easy."

We made a three-point landing,[9-A] almost unnoticeably. The heavy C-46 didn't bounce or sway nor was it necessary to apply brakes. A masterly executed landing.

We turned around and taxied back to the ramp where the trucks waited to unload the cattle. All this was done in total darkness interrupted by the airplane's taxi lights. When we got off the plane we realized that all Changuinola was dark. Our landing had something to do with this. The Curtiss's tail wheel had hooked the high voltage cable and snapped it, leaving the entire Changuinola valley without electricity. It took no time before the police and CLC's Electrical Department employees were demanding explanations.

Captain Prescott was in no mood to answer any questions or explain anything. In a quite undiplomatic and brusque language sprinkled with strong curse words that were self explanatory, he turned his back and left them standing.

The crew spent that night in Changuinola but the next day, as they still hadn't restored the electrical power, the electric fuel pumps weren't working. They decided to cross the Cordillera to David to refuel for their return to their base in Panama City, but not before Captain Prescott let everyone know that he would not be back.

More than half of the cattle remained to be transported. A few days later another Curtiss C-46 from Aero Caribe in Costa Rica arrived to finish the task, but the Panamanian aeronautical authorities forbade the operation, and they didn't make a single flight. It wasn't until a week later that the same Inair C-46 arrived to complete the contract, but this time under the command of Captain Abraham Cholo Castro and Luis Lucho Ameglio as copilot. I didn't participate in the flight more than that first day, but Chiricano did. He had earned his slot as loadmaster.

When commenting to Alcibiades Miranda, the Ganadera Bocas veterinarian, about the bull's behavior during the flight, he assured me that the best thing we could have done was to board those heifers with the bull, because what happened on that flight was a clear case of pheromones. That bull couldn't bear to be separated from his harem.

When I got home, I looked up the definition of the word pheromone in a dictionary and found it to mean: The chemical substance of variable composition that, when sweated by an animal, influences the behavior of others of the same species. Pheromones serve to attract the opposite sex or to mark the territory.

Chapter 10
Formal Instruction

In 1972, nine months after returning from the United Kingdom, Finca Terronal had taken a turn for the worse. The repeated floods had wreaked havoc on the banana production by spreading the parasite nematodes from contaminated farms infecting the soils throughout the Changuinola River basin. Compounding this problem, constant labor confrontations with the newly formed independent banana producers workers union and the rising prices of petroleum products, such as fertilizers, fuel and lubricants after the Organization of the Petroleum Exporting Countries (OPEC) jacked up the crude oil price, made the risk of so large an investment to rehabilitate the farm unfavorable, so the family decided to close banana operations in Changuinola.

While still in Changuinola and evaluating the options I had for the future of my new family, in addition to a wife, I also had a child; I saw an ad in the newspaper for a hydrologist position with the Panama Canal Company (PCC) in Panama City. I felt this was an opportunity I couldn't pass up. In addition to a well-paid job, during my off time I could enroll in a formal flight school and finally obtain my licenses. I was hired, and my plan was that within two years I could be ready to make the jump to my career of choice, aviation.

I made my inquiries and enrolled in the Escuela Aerea in Paitilla, dubbed "La Escuelita" by the students and managed by Captain Isauro Carrizo. I had known Captain Carrizo when he was flying Rapsa DC-3s in Changuinola.

Now, by properly fulfilling all requirements: psychological, cardiovascular, ophthalmological, and auditory evaluations, and doing laboratory and antinarcotics tests that the DAC required to apply for my student license, I was on my way to a proper aviation career. However, I still had to take ground classes before I could take the written exams and, if I passed, then I could start my private pilot flight lessons. Nothing as simple as my initial apprenticeship in Changuinola, but hey, that's the way it had to be.

La Escuelita had four basic training aircraft, but for no fewer than twenty-one wanna-be pilots. The Human Resources Formation Institute (IFARHU) had recently included pilot training in its scholarship program, making it affordable for qualified individuals interested in making aviation a career. My flight schedule was limited to hours after work in PCC and on Saturdays and Sundays, but the demand for aircraft and instructors was such that at that rate, it would take me thirteen months to accumulate the hours necessary to meet the 40-hour requirement for a private pilot's license. Not to mention the commercial license and the instrument and multi-engine ratings.

While airplane gazing in Paitilla with the family one weekend, I noticed an airplane parked in an open hangar. It was for sale. In those days there were no restrictions to accessing the hangars. It was a 1954 Cessna 170B, similar to the one Vanolli operated back in the days in Sixaola: a 4-seater taildragger. HP-374. I knew instantly that this was the solution to get my license without the constant frustrations experienced in La Escuelita: The plane's booked; the plane was taken by another student and hasn't returned; the plane's in maintenance; the plane's under inspection; the plane's waiting for parts, and the multiple other setbacks of most every aviation school. The asking price for the Cessna was USD $3,500.00 including an open hangar. I spoke with the owner, Captain Bill Bailey, a Canal pilot, who had used it for traveling back and forth to a mountain house he had in Cerro Punta. He was selling it because he had retired and was leaving Panama. I got a loan with Citibank that took more than a month for approval, a lot longer than the one-day transaction that I had made in Changuinola to buy the Aeronca.

Since I already had taildragger flying time, though I couldn't legally include those hours in my logbook, I asked Captain Carrizo to check me out in the 170. We agreed that he would demonstrate what maneuvers I needed to learn for my check ride, and I would practice them on my own. He had begun his career flying 170s on the Azuero Peninsula, so he conveyed the tips for getting the maximum performance out of a 170. That I liked. I managed to rack up the required flight hours and in no time was ready for my private pilot check ride. Captain Osman Valderrama was the DAC examining pilot and all went according to plan. I passed. Now I had to accumulate the remaining 200 hours for my commercial license, including twenty-five solo night hours and ten hours cross-country. In one month I got my night hours; I would take off from Paitilla before sunset, and fly over the area of the city for two to three hours depending on the weather, and then to Tocumen to land where my wife Pat and my son Teo were waiting to drive me home. In those days Paitilla didn't have runway lights. The next day, the same routine but this time I would take off from Tocumen and return, until I managed to log twenty-five hours solo night hours, one step nearer to my commercial license.

With my private license, I could legally take passengers and at every opportunity, I would fly the 170 on family outings. We traveled all over Panama: to the San Blas islands in the Caribbean, the Perlas Islands in the Pacific, the Darien, Chiriqui and of course, Bocas and even to San Jose, Costa Rica. Once I logged my 200 hours and passed the written commercial exam, I was signed off for the commercial flight exam. The DAC examiner was Captain Aulio Hernandez, with whom I had started my instruction in Almirante five years before. Although he had a reputation for being a demanding examiner, I passed my check-ride without much trauma. I was well honed for it. I was finally a licensed commercial pilot.

So what now? I had a commercial license, but I was limited to flying passengers only within a 50-mile radius. I needed a flight instrument rating, a certification that authorizes the pilot to fly in instrument meteorological conditions solely by instrument reference as ordained by Instrument Flight Rules, IFR. A regulation, prompted by the DAC after a series of accidents caused by non-instrument-rated pilots inadvertently entering adverse weather conditions, required pilots to be instrument-rated for commercial flights. In addition to that, in order to qualify as a copilot for companies that operated transport category aircraft weighing more than 12,500 pounds, a multi-engine rating was also required. To obtain either rating requires a sizeable sum of money. It's necessary to train with a certified instructor in an aircraft equipped for instrument flight for a minimum of 15 hours, and for the multi-engine rating, training is in a multi-engine aircraft with an appropriate instructor for a minimum of 10 hours of instruction. The airplane and the instruction for these two ratings are significantly more expensive than those required for basic training. And to apply for a flying job with Copa, the most important airline in those days, candidates had to have 1,500 hours flight time, of which 500 were to be in a turbine-powered airplane. Apart from the fact that vacancies were few and sporadic, since I was employed and already had a university degree, the IFARHU was out of consideration. Besides, at age 27, I exceeded the maximum qualifying age, so once again I was stuck in space. But I did have a big advantage. I had an airplane. Now the question was how to accumulate that large number of hours and obtain the required ratings.

Above 1: The Aeronca 7AC, Ibu's first airplane with his first passenger, his dad, Teofilo Alvarado, Changuinola, Panama, 1969.

Above 2: The teacher from Almirante and her friend Rosa Amador in front of the Aeronca 7AC. Changuinola, Panama, 1970.

Above: Aerolíneas Urraca DC-3, Enrique Malek Airport, David, Chiriqui, Panama.

Above 1: Inair's Curtiss Commando C-46, HP-483, that transported cattle from Rio Hato to Changuinola in 1971.
© Germinal Sarasqueta.

Above 2: Alas Chiricanas DC-3. Enrique Malek Airport, David, Chiriqui, Panama.

Above 3: Ibu meets up with the Aeronca 7AC after twenty years. Enrique Malek Airport, David, Chiriqui, Panama, 1990.

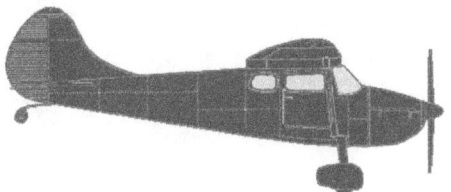

Part 4
Licensed Pilot

11 Learning by Doing
12 Exotic Species
13 Get-home-itis
14 Unconventional Check Airman
15 Back Seat Jockey
16 Cloud Seeding
17 Splashdown in Nargana

Chapter 11
Learning by Doing

While at La Escuelita, I met Gustavo Tato Cuervo, who serviced and maintained the school's aircraft. Once I acquired the 170, I approached Tato with the offer to be his assistant when the 170 needed work and annual inspections. This arrangement enabled me primarily to acquire the basic knowledge required for maintaining single-engine aircraft and considerably reduced my maintenance costs.

But the problem of accumulating flight hours was my continual dilemma and I still hadn't found a solution. Flying just to fly, even though enjoyable, didn't make much sense. I had to find a way to justify and, more importantly, financially sustain these flights.

I was in Paitilla one afternoon when Constantino Tinito Romero, a colorful and respected pilot who owned a bush flying operation, suddenly approached me: "Ibu, I need to take a battery to El Porvenir. I have a stranded plane. I'll provide the gasoline."

I jumped at that offer since it was an opportunity to earn flight hours. That trip that afternoon to El Porvenir in the San Blas islands was a one-of-a-kind flight for me. It was already late afternoon when we left so there was pressure to return before they closed the Paitilla airport. While we were still ascending to get above the cloud tops, Tinito emphatically insisted that he had a route that saved at least ten minutes of flight time. His would cross the mountain range at its lowest point by entering the Madroño Valley at 1,500 feet. That's what we did. We flew between layers of clouds following the Madroño riverbed and ended up over Carti, on the Caribbean coast. We could see El Porvenir Island a few miles ahead. When we landed, Tinito jumped out with the spare battery for his stranded C-185, and I immediately took off and headed for Panama City. Yes, this time at a safe and comfortable altitude of 4,500 feet. I had no desire to scud-run in unfamiliar mountainous areas.

The flight that day opened the doors for me to accumulate my long sought-after flight hours since Tinito offered to register my plane in his company Transporte Aéreo Tinito S.A. (Tatsa) and fly special flights when his two Cessna 185s were occupied or out of service. Of course I accepted. I would accept any opportunity to fly and accumulate hours. I was back on track to achieve my goal. And also, I thought, I might eventually end up flying one of Tinito's powerful 185s. Tinito joked that his pilots had to be featherweights. That way he could carry more payload, which meant more profits. I weighed 150 pounds, so in that respect, I qualified. I was excited and motivated.

Even though my payment while flying for Tatsa in my own airplane was in avgas, I was able to accumulate not only hours, but also valuable experience. That was my real compensation. The areas where I usually had to fly, Darien and San Blas, were marginal to say the least, without navigational, communication or radar coverage. The flying was solely by pilotage, which is flying by reference to the visible landmarks or checkpoints and by dead reckoning, which is by computations based on time, speed, distance and direction. There wasn't a Saturday or Sunday that I wasn't called to do some odd flight. All of them were experience-building and unique.

Chapter 12
Exotic Species

One Monday afternoon Tinito called to ask me to go to Hotel Ideal to meet with Gary, a Californian who exported exotic species from his base in Darien. That night when I met with Gary, he outlined his needs for my services. I was to fly at dawn on Saturday to El Real, a jungle community on the banks of the Chucunaque River deep in the Darien jungle. We would load the plane with the animal species of the day, and I would return to Tocumen Airport in time to ship them on a KLM flight to Amsterdam, Netherlands. The 170 should be configured without passenger seats so that 12 cardboard boxes, specially designed to fit on a single-engine plane, could be loaded.

That Saturday, I was at Paitilla before daybreak. The 170 was full of gasoline, without passenger seats and ready to go. I started the engine and taxied to line up with all the other bush pilots, *Silvestres*, as they were known locally. As soon as the airport was officially open, the tower operator authorized takeoffs by "first call, first off." It was mayhem trying to get the tower to acknowledge your call. Once in the air, Panama Control Center, administered by the Federal Aviation Administration (FAA), would partially control the flights. Radar coverage didn't include Darien or San Blas where most of these aircraft were headed. So, fifty miles out, aircraft separation was based solely on "see and be seen." En route, I could hear the different pilots giving their estimated position, course and altitude in the blind, meant for all others on the frequency. I quickly realized that with no air traffic control coverage, they were keeping themselves separated. There was constant chatter as they navigated in and out of clouds, and an eagle-eye lookout was vital. It was instrument flying on a visual flight plan. However, if it wasn't done this way, it's doubtful any flights could be completed, especially during the rainy season. I'd been warned that at that time of the morning, a layer of fog generally blankets the jungle canopy and doesn't dissipate until the sun begins to warm the ground.

Abeam La Palma, capital of Darien province, at the mouth of the Chucunaque River, the planned route was to continue upriver until I spotted the community of El Real. Once I left the coastline, I could see that the fog hadn't dissipated over the dense canopy and that it covered the entire landmass, including the river. I flew down on the river deck and selected partial flaps to increase lift and allow the plane to fly slower, carefully turning left and right as the river meandered between the trees. All this time I was paying close attention to the radio just in case another plane was doing the same but in the opposite direction. I had picked up this technique from the other student pilots during BS sessions sitting on the "DC-6," as the long wooden bench in front of La Escuelita was known and where it was rumored that many of the students' logbook hours were actually recorded. So, after about thirty minutes of slow and low turns flying over the deck, I spotted the village of El Real, then the runway on the opposite right river bank. Since El Real de Santa Maria in Darien had been founded in colonial times, I thought I was going to find a village with cobblestone streets and a chapel in the middle of a square, something like Panama La Vieja. What I saw when I approached the runway were a few dozen zinc-roofed houses, another dozen thatched-roofed ones and wooden planks instead of cobblestones. Nothing like what I had envisioned. I felt a bit disappointed, but I was already on final with the airplane configured for landing, so I didn't distract myself with past history. I went straight in and landed on a muddy grass field.

Gary was waiting for me with several cardboard boxes with small breathing orifices that were stamped with the legend, Exotic Species. When I asked Gary about it, he assured me they were reptiles. We got busy loading the boxes and dropped the subject. They had been packed at dawn and should be kept in the shade until loaded on the flight to Amsterdam, Gary cautioned.

"Sure. In one hour forty-five minutes I'll be at Tocumen Airport delivering them," I replied, feeling confident.

As soon as I was airborne with my exotic cargo, I could see La Palma and further away, the Perlas archipelago. The ground fog had burned off by then and the visibility was unlimited. I ascended to a comfortable altitude of 4,500 feet and settled down to enjoy the flight. It was 9:30 a.m., and the morning was cool. Suddenly I heard a sliding noise inside the cardboard box at the top of the stack where the copilot's seat is normally located. The box was next to my face. I was startled and tried to move, but the safety belt coupled with the shoulder harness held me firmly in place. I could see a tiny pair of eyes peeping through one of the holes. My only recourse was to lean as far as possible on the left side of the cabin to get away from that box.

That return trip was one of the most stressful that I remember in my short experience. During that never-ending flight, I kept thinking, if that reptile is a snake, it could slither through the holes in the box and end up loose on the cabin floor, so I placed the heels of my feet on top of the rudder pedals, just in case.

When I finally landed at Tocumen, the boxes were unloaded and I returned to Paitilla, happy and relieved to have achieved the flight without major consequences, but I resolved to find out exactly what my load would be before accepting to carry it from then on.

From the time I had left my house at 5:00 that morning, I had invested almost eight hours and had only managed to log three and a half flight hours. However, thinking positively, besides having received 20 gallons of avgas for what the airplane consumed, I had flown to a remote and historical place I had never been before and to top it off, I had added more flight time to my experience. How could I complain about such a good arrangement?

The next Saturday, Gary assured me that what I had flown on that first flight was not snakes but lizards. That clarification reassured me. The Saturday routine continued for a few weeks until the Saturday that the boxes contained baby parakeets. There were 24 per box, and when the Tocumen Airport customs agents inspected the boxes in my presence, more than half had died. They had no water, and some still had their eyes closed they were so young. That scene was so impacting that right then I decided to end those flights. I found out later that the Darien local custom for capturing parakeets is by chopping down the trees where their nests are detected. Through this uncivilized and anti-environmental practice, the survival rate of those recently hatched birds is very low.

A few months later, the Directorate of Renewable Natural Resources (RENARE) began to enforce a provision that was already established by law that protected wildlife against this type of operation, that is, the export of wild species without official control or permission. I like to think that my conversation about this pitiful situation with the RENARE director at that time, Ricardo Gutierrez, had something to do with it. Last I heard about Gary was that he had left Panama and gone to Brazil. I guess to continue in his commercial trading. My days of flying exotic species were short in duration, but big in amassed experience.

Chapter 13
Get-home-itis

The flights I undertook for Tatsa were always interesting experiences, to say the least, and in some cases more than I would have liked, especially the one that happened on a Friday afternoon. I got an urgent call from Tatsa's receptionist requesting that I make a flight to El Porvenir to take a bilge pump for a sailboat that was in San Blas. Of course I agreed. When I got to Paitilla it was after five in the afternoon. The estimated time on the route was thirty minutes there and about thirty-five minutes back, so I couldn't delay the takeoff. Since there were no runway lights at Paitilla Airport then, I had to be back before the airport closed. I fueled up and took off in record time. I used Tinito's route through the Madroño Valley to save time, but I was not happy doing it.

When I landed in El Porvenir, I back taxied the plane to the end of the strip where the sailboat owner was waiting for his precious part, and without turning off the engine, I handed him the bilge pump and bid farewell. As I applied power and at the same time applied right brake to align the 170 with the short strip, I felt the brake pedal go all the way to the bottom without any braking effect on that wheel, and the plane veered to the left, a result of the engine torque. I had lost the right wheel brake, the critical one for a tail wheel airplane. Shit, it can't be!

I tried a couple of times to apply gradual power to see if I could roll in a straight line down the track, but to no avail. I was stuck in El Porvenir for the night and would have to wait to get help from Paitilla the next day. There was simply no other option. There was no telephone or radio in El Porvenir so I couldn't inform Panama that I would remain over night on the island. All of a sudden, while sitting on the tire, I came up with an idea that might remedy this situation: What if someone ran next to the airplane and held the tail's horizontal stabilizer preventing it from swinging to the right and thus keep the plane's nose from turning left? That, in turn, would allow the airplane to roll down the runway in a straight line and, when it reached sufficient speed and the rudder would become effective, I could then continue the take-off. Brilliant solution!

Right then I recruited a volunteer from the several islanders who had gathered around and I carefully explained the operation. Once I was sure the volunteer had understood the instructions, I jumped in the plane and started the engine. I gradually pushed the throttle forward and felt the plane moving in a straight line, the result of the force applied by my unseen recruit on the tail's horizontal stabilizer. We're making progress, good, I thought. The ground speed increased rapidly and just when I neared the speed required to raise the tail, I felt a blunt jolt and the nose swing to the left a bit. The tail rudder seemed somewhat effective, so I continued to roll slightly skewed until I was able to straighten it by applying full right pedal, which controls the rudder. As soon as I felt I had minimum speed for lift-off, I applied full flaps and managed to make the plane fly; barely, but it was off the ground. A few seconds later, after slowly retracting flaps, I began a shallow climb, then I circled the runway to see what had caused the sudden jar at the start of the takeoff roll. Flying from a height of about 50 feet, I saw my recruit stretched out on the ground. His friends were waving their arms at me, indicating that he was okay, and for me to leave. I then realized what had happened. Instead of grabbing the horizontal stabilizer by its side, my volunteer had stood in front of the stabilizer and run backwards, so as the plane rapidly picked up speed, the stabilizer hit him in the stomach and knocked him down. But hey, he was probably bruised a bit, but he was okay.

I climbed with a southwest heading to cross the San Blas mountain range toward the Pacific coast. The sun was beginning to set, and I knew that I wouldn't be able to get to Paitilla before dark. That's when I realized how stupid I had been. Taking off in an airplane with problems at that time of the afternoon was not smart. Why the rush to get to Paitilla? Worse yet, the airport would be closed and I'd be committing a serious violation if I attempted to land in the dark. But I was stuck, because I couldn't return to El Porvenir and land on that narrow short and dark runway without my critical right brake. What do I do now? Again, with that incredible lack of mental dexterity I was experiencing that day, I decided not to declare an emergency, but instead to go directly to the Gamboa airport located on the banks of the Panama Canal. It had a long grass runway, and I was familiar with it since I instructed from it. Also, there were no aeronautical authorities to answer to. But, like Paitilla and El Porvenir, it didn't have runway lights.

It was a clear night and when I crossed over the mountains, I could see the Pacific coast, the lights of Panama City and in the distance, the red and green buoy lights aligning the Canal. Gamboa was to my right at the northern entrance of the Culebra Cut. This runway had a high-voltage cable on its south approach end and to the side, Cerro Pelado, a hilltop with communication antennae towers well defined with bright flashing lights. I circled the runway, relieved that the buoy lights were parallel to the runway. I made a high and very slow approach, with the high voltage cables in mind. With one inoperative brake, I was not going to be able to use the other functioning one to keep me rolling in a straight line when touching down. Although the 170 had landing lights, I could not see the windsock to determine how the wind was blowing and could only hope it was a calm night with no crosswinds. I'd have to let it roll without braking until inertia stopped it. That's how it went. I descended gradually with little power and full flaps. The Stall Warning horn kept blaring, indicating that I was 5 mph above a stall. Pum, Pum, was all I heard when the 170 settled firmly on the grass runway. It rolled a few feet and stopped. I cut the engine and sat for several minutes without moving, thinking: I've been in this predicament before. Of course, in the Aeronca flight from Almirante to Changuinola many years ago. That time I had sworn I wouldn't allow myself to get in a situation like this ever again. But here I was, having had another scare that I alone had caused. Thinking back, perhaps the night landing with Captain Prescott in the Inair Curtiss C-46 in Changuinola taught me the importance of keeping calm and concentrating on the situation: Slow it down, easy does it, easy, easy.

In aviation there is an expression called "Get-home-itis," and there are few aviators who haven't found themselves in similar settings. This weakness, in the absence of good judgment, occurs on return flights where the pilots do everything possible to return to their base of operation. Many times decisions are made that, if it had been on the departure flight, would never have been considered. This was the case with me that afternoon at the El Porvenir airport. I had felt compelled to get home, no matter what.

Chapter 14
Unconventional Check Airman

Very much to my regret, I never got checked out in Tatsa's 185 because the company closed operations after wrecking its two airplanes, but I did manage to get checked out in another 185 by its notorious owner, Jose de Jesus Martinez, aka Chuchu. Chuchu Martinez, a doctor of philosophy, a mathematician, a university professor, a poet, a discotheque owner and pilot, was unorthodox and unique. After actively and openly opposing the 1968 National Guard coup d'état of the Panamanian government, he later became immersed in that same institution with the rank of Corporal. He became General Torrijos's political advisor, and insisted on maintaining his original rank as corporal within the institution. He referred to himself as Corporal Martinez. He was often seen boarding the FAP's Westwind Jet at the Paitilla airport accompanying Torrijos on international missions, but as an adviser, not as part of the crew. He had baptized his Cessna 185 as the ALEPH I, most likely because of its mathematical or philosophical significance. Chuchu's peculiarity as an instructor pilot was that he instructed from the left seat, the seat usually reserved for the student, since the main flight instruments are on that side.[14-A] Switching sides to fly can be extremely difficult for some pilots if they aren't used to it. Such was the case with Chuchu. He wasn't comfortable instructing from the right side. It was a known fact among pilots in Paitilla. Chuchu's line was that it was advantageous for the student to receive instruction on the right side because it would be helpful when he became an instructor pilot. I didn't go for that story, but then again, it was his plane, and since I wanted to get checked out in a 185, I didn't refute his explanation. Since I was already an instructor, I was used to flying on the right side, so it was not a problem. On reflection, it wasn't really a check ride at all, but rather a joy ride, because I received no instruction nor was I given any pertinent information.

At the end of the flight, Chuchu's parting words were: "Now you're ready to instruct in a 185."

I thanked him and walked away doubtful about the whole procedure. But I did take off and land the plane three times in accordance with the regulations to be considered current in the airplane. Current if I had already been checked out in the plane, but I hadn't, so I didn't fall into that category, but I flew it and on paper a certified instructor checked me out. On paper yes, but not in real life.

A few months later Chuchu wrecked his C-185 while landing on one of the short runways at San Blas, and that was the end of ALEPH I.

Chapter 15
Back Seat Jockey

Flying as a passenger also provides interesting experiences or lessons, such as the one on a Sahsa flight from New Orleans to San Pedro Sula in 1977.

After a brief stay in the US, at which time I got my FAA commercial license, I scheduled a visit on the return trip to San Pedro Sula, Honduras, to visit Jorge and Carol Montealegre. Jorge, a Nicaraguan, had been a college classmate and was now a Bank of America manager, assigned to San Pedro Sula.

The flight was announced to leave at two in the afternoon, but it was already five o'clock and we were still waiting in the terminal at Moisant Airport. The Sahsa agents at the counter assured us that the delay would be brief, but it wasn't until after six when they announced that we could board the flight. The airplane was a Boeing 737. What happened to the Lockheed Electra Turbo props that Sahsa operated?

The plane was full, and among the passengers were some sport fishermen who were in a festive mood from the many cocktails they had had at the bar during the long wait. When the airplane finally initiated its takeoff run, and after what seemed like an eternity, its nose lifted, but it was immediately lowered back on the runway. It continued rolling with its nose down and again there was an attempt to lift off, but you could feel it was wobbly as it picked up speed. Near the end of the runway, it flew, half-heartedly, but it flew. The cabin was deadly quiet except for the whine of the engines as we climbed. Not far below, we could see the waters of Lake Pontchartrain.

The trip was routine with excellent on-board service. Night fell soon, and around two and a half hours into the flight we were descending towards San Pedro Sula. The sea was dark, but we could see the lights of the houses on the coast as the engines were powered back. We were low, but neither the landing gear nor the flaps were deployed. The 737 turned back towards the sea again and entered a holding pattern, a procedure exercised when there are delays for bad weather over the airport or because of traffic density, but in this case the night was clear and what air traffic could there be in San Pedro Sula at this time of night?

We had been circling a little over an hour before the 737 started to fly back towards the coast and we heard the landing gear go down and the flaps extending.

"Here it comes, we're lining up to land," I told Teo who was sitting next to me.

Through the window we could see that we were inland. The Ramón Villeda Morales Airport, which serves the city of San Pedro Sula, is located in La Lima and is surrounded by banana plantations. We could see the runway threshold lights passing under the plane's wings and the lights on the edge of the runway quickly fleeting by, way too fast for my comfort, but still the tires hadn't touched ground. We were coming in hot. I could feel the plane floating. We must have passed the runway's halfway point when suddenly the plane lowered its nose and all wheels struck the tarmac firmly. The pilot immediately began applying the brakes and reverse to both turbines. The plane swung from side to side, with a downward tilt. The cabin lights blinked off and on. The overhead compartments opened and briefcases, packages, and purses began to fall. The emergency oxygen masks fell and hung over our faces. People were shouting and screaming hysterically. Even the cabin attendants looked terrified. It wasn't until the aircraft finally stopped that we all breathed with relief. What a scare for everyone, and I'm sure we could include the pilots, too!

Jorge and Carol were waiting for us at the terminal and after the greetings and hugs, Jorge's first words were: "*Jodido*, what luck you have! You've just been on Sahsa's first jet airline flight and the first night landing at San Pedro Sula airport!"

The next morning the newspaper headlines read: "*Catrachos* Inaugurate the Jet Era." The article went on to say that the *Catracho* (Honduran) crew had picked up the brand new 737 at the Boeing factory in Seattle, Washington, and flown it to San Pedro. It was the first airplane to land at night at the airport. New aircraft deliveries by the manufacturers normally provide the crews a complete course in the aircraft systems, and instruction is provided in a flight simulator that responds to the airplane model.[15-A] So, there was the possibility that the flight from the factory to San Pedro Sula, with a stopover in New Orleans, was the first time the crew commanded a 737 in real time. Whew! And to top it off, that night the airport was inaugurating its runway lights system. So, it was the first time anyone had landed there at night, experienced crew or not. The airport didn't have a precision Instrument Landing System (ILS), a ground-based navigational aid that indicates lateral and vertical orientation all the way to touchdown. Therefore that approach was performed only with the aid of a Very High Frequency Omnidirectional Range (VOR), which gives only horizontal orientation, a non-precision landing. I shuddered a little with that analysis and decided it was better not to dwell on the subject. Anyway, the flight had ended satisfactorily, with a stiff dose of fright, of course. (Pucker Factor = 10)

To date, when we fly together as passengers as a family on an airline and the landing is less than perfect, we laugh and remember that Sahsa inaugural flight in San Pedro Sula. *Jodido!*

Chapter 16
Cloud Seeding

In 1983, both the Panama Canal Commission (PCC) and Panama's Institute of Hydraulic Resources and Electrification (IRHE) faced a water emergency. The prolonged dry season had affected the Canal operations to the point that drafts of transiting ships had to be restricted due to the low water levels in Gatun Lake. In Lake Bayano the levels were also so low that the IRHE was considering instituting programmed nationwide daily blackouts. At the end of April of that year, the PCC requested technical assistance from the US Department of the Interior Bureau of Reclamation (USDI-BR), experienced in researching methods of drought attenuation for years.[16-A] The USDI-BR recommended a program that consisted of using aircraft to seed clouds with chemicals and other techniques to stimulate rain.

Dr. Wallace Howell was the expert scientist who came on behalf of the USDI-BR. His initial mission was to present the uncertainties, risks and benefits involved in cloud seeding to the PCC and the IRHE. Both institutions decided to proceed. I was assigned by PCC to coordinate with the DAC authorities for the corresponding flight permits. Wally, as he insisted he be called, was an octogenarian meteorologist and also an experienced pilot who was still flying his private Beechcraft Bonanza plane. He was a unique character. On one occasion, right before we entered a meeting with Victor Cruz, IRHE's Director General, and my brother Pao, who was the Operations Director, Wally led me aside and whispered, "Let's not lie, but let's not tell them all we know, and above all, let's go pee so we can negotiate without pressure."

And so it was, the meeting was carried out satisfactorily for both parties, with the commitment that a third of the flights would cover IRHE's Bayano Lake basin, even though PCC would be contributing ninety percent of the cost, which was three hundred twenty-five thousand dollars (US $325,000.00). The ten percent that the IRHE promised to pay was, according to Wally, only symbolic; he felt it was important for them to feel identified with the project and support when the inevitable government bureaucracy took hold. Sure enough, right before the project began, DAC opposed granting us a reserved air space between 10,000 – 20,000 feet over the areas to fly. It was IRHE that managed to obtain the approval for reserving that airspace for us when requested.

The cloud seeding team that arrived consisted of four pilots; two of the four were a South African married couple. The two airplanes to be used were a Piper Navajo and a Beechcraft Baron each modified to carry four different types of dispersing apparatus: a silver iodide flare firing system, an ammonium iodide smoke generator with acetone, a solid carbon dioxide (dry ice) dispenser and a fine hygroscopic solution consisting of ammonium nitrate and urea dispenser. Each of these configurations would be applied depending on the type of cloud.

The operation consisted of using the PCC's meteorological radar to vector the airplanes to the area of clouds loaded with water in suspension. These clouds traveled following the longitudinal axis of the Canal watershed from northeast to southwest. In general, the core of these cumulonimbus clouds ranged from 18,000 to 25,000 feet in altitude. Two pilots were assigned to each airplane and took turns either piloting or communicating with the ground personnel and maneuvering to keep circulating inside the cloud. A third important crewmember was in charge of tending to the corresponding dispersing systems. The base of operations was Paitilla airport and on the second day after arrival, one of the pilots had to return to the US because of amoebas probably caught on one of the stopovers of the flight down to Panama. The lack of a pilot problem had a quick and easy solution since both Wally and I were licensed pilots and could perform that task while waiting for a replacement. Meanwhile, the other pilots not flying could take turns doing the chemical dispensing until we could recruit someone to permanently fill the position.

Originally, I had expected to recruit from among the unemployed pilots who were prowling the airport looking for an opportunity to fly. Even though they wouldn't be able to log flying hours, they would get some unique experience just from being aboard a cloud seeding airplane, I thought. Well, it didn't pan out that way. We weren't able to recruit anyone because the word had already spread that the flights consisted of more than an hour circling inside a cumulonimbus in severe turbulence, with outside temperature around −10°C and lightning strikes that could make you jump off your seat when they hit the plane. Come to think of it, maybe I wouldn't have gotten into this either if it weren't for the affection that I had for flying. During a flight in the middle of severe turbulence, I turned to ask Jim, the other pilot on that flight, if the planes had any kind of structural reinforcement for this type of flying. His answer was a simple: "Nope." Not exactly the answer I was looking for, for sure.

No one expressed desire to join the team except Mr.

Dorcey, a well known person around Paitilla, who, although neither pilot, nor mechanic, nor airplane owner, was accepted in the closed Paitilla circle. He had a scrap metal and dump truck business, and could be found most afternoons at the airport hoping to be invited to fly. One afternoon he approached me and let me know that he would be interested in applying for the crew vacancy in the cloud seeding project. I talked it over with the rest of the crew. There was some reluctance to hire him mainly because of his advanced age, but hell, Wally was about the same age and Wally was doing just fine. He would have to do. That settled it; we could now reschedule the flights to be less arduous on the pilots having to also perform as dispensers.

That same afternoon Mr. Dorcey's job duties were discussed with him and he was walked through on how each of the on-board systems operated and shown how to don the oxygen mask after passing through 12,000 feet since neither airplane was pressurized.[16-B]

The next day around noon, we were notified by radio that several cumulonimbus clouds were spotted approaching the Canal watershed so we immediately proceeded to meet them and begin the operation. When we were approaching 12,000 feet, I turned around and motioned for Dorcey to put on his mask. We reached the cloud base at about 16,000 feet, and could see it was rapidly building up. Once inside, everything darkened, and the turbulence took over and soon we could hear the heavy raindrops as they struck the aluminum fuselage. Jim was fighting hard to keep the Navajo in the center of the cell by holding the wings in a steep bank. The turbulence was so severe that it became difficult to communicate with the air traffic controller and the meteorologist operating the radar in Balboa. The autopilot was out of the question. We took turns at the control every ten minutes. With each lightning strike, the outside was immediately illuminated as if someone had suddenly turned on the stadium lights. The most impressive thing was when a lightning bolt would hit the plane. One felt the electricity traveling through the fuselage towards static dischargers. Wherever lightning struck, it would leave a small pin size hole in the leading edge of the wing and where the electricity was discharged in the trailing edge, it left a hole an inch in diameter of melted aluminum. What's this? Pilots usually do everything possible to avoid rotten weather like this and here we were doing our best to remain right in the middle of it.

After about thirty minutes in the middle of the cluster, I happened to look back to see how Dorcey was doing. What I saw startled me. He was lying on the floor with his eyes closed. I signaled Jim we were cancelling the operation and pointed to Dorcey who was lying on the floor. Jim maneuvered out of the clouds and began an emergency descent. Once out of the turbulence, I was able to unbuckle my seatbelt and see about Dorcey. I took his mask off and he was breathing but his face was completely blue and he was unconscious. Before landing, we called for an ambulance, which was waiting to attend to Dorcey and take him to the hospital. Once the initial crisis was over, I went back to the plane to see what might have happened and found the mask hose not completely plugged in the oxygen socket. At no time had he inhaled oxygen. It was a clear case of hypoxia.[16-C] One of the dangers of flying for more than thirty minutes above 12,000 feet without supplemental oxygen is that you lose consciousness.

We didn't see Dorcey again for several weeks, so Wally

and I again took turns performing third crewman duties until I hired Francis who had done odd gardening jobs for me around the house to fill in. He remained the official dispenser throughout the project doing an excellent job.

The operation began on May 31 and ended on August 27, 1983. Sixty-one days were flown. As for the project itself, the effectiveness achieved depends on who's asked, but the fact is that to have a result based on scientific data, a lot more data would have been needed than what those sixty-one days provided. As for me personally, both while flying and on the ground, I didn't perceive any increase in the amount of rain during that period. The lakes didn't increase their water levels and it wasn't until November, normally late rainy season, when the rains began. I think it was a simple case of nature refusing to be manipulated by man.

Chapter 17
Splashdown in Nargana

With a couple of hundred flight hours in the 170, I felt I knew everything I should know about the plane. I still had not heard that wise saying about every flight being a learning experience.

In those days there was a huge demand to supply restaurants and hotels in Panama City with fresh lobsters from San Blas. Flying lobsters carried a certain amount of risk mainly for operating at maximum takeoff weight under less than ideal runway conditions, and the unpredictable inclement weather was also a factor to reckon with. I don't recall how I ended up doing those lobster flights, since the business end of it didn't interest me and they were for a third party. Logging flight hours was a key factor for me.

That particular day I took off early from Paitilla with only the front seats to pick up a load of lobsters waiting for me in Nargana, a small island on the Caribbean coast. The mountain range was covered over with cloud, but that was about par for that time of the year. What concerned me were the dark clouds to the north, offshore, which indicated thunderstorms and heavy rain. As it was early, my plan was to land, load and take off before the bad weather arrived, which could be a torrential downpour with poor visibility and strong crosswinds that make normal takeoffs and landings somewhat precarious.

When I landed in Nargana, some divers still hadn't returned with their catch of live lobsters. I waited anxiously eyeing the storm approaching in the distance. Just as the plane was finally loaded, it started to rain, but there was still enough visibility to see the other end of the narrow sand strip 1200 feet long. I had already started the engine and was checking the magnetos when I noticed one of the native fishermen waving his arms signaling me to wait. He wanted me to take the *sáhila*, a Kuna chief, to Panama City. I reluctantly agreed. I also accepted a dozen beautiful blue crabs, which I assumed was a token of appreciation for accepting to fly the *sáhila*. I tossed the sack into the back of the plane, buckled down my passenger and proceeded to line up with the strip. Then I selected 20° of flaps and applied all the power available to the 145 horsepower engine. It took a few seconds to start rolling, but as we picked up speed, there were moments when it seemed to slow down, as if I were applying the brakes. I realized that the few minutes of heavy rain had formed puddles of water that were making the takeoff run more cumbersome. It wasn't the first time I had taken off from Nargana with similar weight, or with rain, but I had never taken off in such a heavy downpour and a waterlogged runway.

Three-quarters down the runway I still hadn't reached takeoff speed. I knew the strip ended abruptly with a six-foot drop onto a coral reef, so aborting the takeoff at that point would be risky. Trying to stop the airplane in these wet conditions would mean skidding on the muddy ground and most probably I wouldn't be able to stop the plane before the end of the runway. I made an instant decision to continue the takeoff and if I still didn't have the flying airspeed by the time I reached the end, I'd apply full flaps to force the plane to fly with ground effect. I had done just that a few months before, when I had flown two heavy jungle trekkers and their gear out of the Nombre de Dios grass strip during an emergency extraction. On that occasion I had flown under ground effect just above the water for about a mile until the airplane's speed crept up enough to retract flaps and climb.

So as I approached the end of the runway, I applied full 40° flaps; and the 170 responded as expected, ballooning. It was barely dangling on, but it was flying. Then right at the end of the runway, where the ground dropped off and there was no solid surface under the wings, the ground effect was lost and the plane started to sink, but it kept flying just above the surface. Now it was a matter of gradually retracting the flaps to increase the speed and start a slow climb. We were making progress, when suddenly the engine started sputtering and coughing. Shit! Rainwater had entered the carburetor. I immediately pulled the carb heat control and within seconds the coughing stopped, but valuable engine revolutions were lost because of the hot air from the exhaust being fed to the carburetor fuel-air mixture. I knew then that the 170 would not keep flying and that we would hit the water.

On reflection, I think that at that moment, intuitively, I went into emergency mode and began preparation for a water landing. Only a few days before, on a flight over the Gulf of Panama, a pilot friend, Bob Deimert, had briefed me on emergency water landings. Bob was a Canadian whose business was to retrieve World War II aircraft from the jungle or bottom of the seas wherever in the world they had wrecked, and restore them to sell to aviation museums. That day of our conversation on water landings, we were going to inspect the remains of an abandoned airplane that had been covered by the jungle next to the Jaque runway in Darien, near the Colombian border. We were flying over the Gulf of Panama at 5,500 feet when Bob asked me if I thought we could make it to the mainland if we had an engine failure. I did some mental calculations based on the distance from the coast and altitude we were at and I answered no. He then shared with me his experience flying in Canada, where there are thousands of bodies of water. If ditching of a fixed gear airplane is necessary, Canadian bush pilots have devised a technique to minimize the risk.

Basically, it's a logical technique: Before the impact with the water, open one of the cabin doors and descend slowly with maximum flaps, then just before the tires touch the water, stall the plane and at the same time, maneuver the airplane with full right rudder to get the right wing to be the first thing that hits the water. This maneuver swings the plane to the right, incrusting the nose in the water, with the sole purpose of preventing it from turning over, or flipping. This way, the occupants don't end up upside down, disoriented and trapped inside the cabin unable to exit until the cabin is equalized with the external water pressure that would then allow them to open the door.

That's what I did. The 170's wing struck the water and forced the nose into the water and its cabin section in the air and the tail straight up. The *sáhila* and I were hanging from our three-point harness and the bags full of lobsters were all over our backs. The water quickly entered the cabin, and because I had partially opened my door, I was able to push it open to squeeze out. Once floating outside, I realized that my passenger was still inside. Thankfully, the 170 was still floating nose down but it was sinking, so I entered the cabin again to help the *sáhila* get out. He was fighting to undo the harness, a Huey UH-1 military helicopter harness; very different from the Paitilla aircraft seatbelts he was used to. Those 3-point harnesses prevented our faces from smashing against the instrument panel in that sudden stop. I quickly released the harness buckle and dragged him out just before the 170 regurgitated and sank in slow motion. All this time it was raining hard and the shore was not visible, but apparently the *sáhila* was well oriented because he began to swim, and I quickly lost sight of him. For some bizarre reason, I chose to stay with the plane while it sank, at times trying to keep it afloat. I remember thinking: This can't be happening. I'm a cautious pilot; the airplane's in good mechanical condition; I'm a good human being; I don't hold a grudge against anyone. This can't be. I must be dreaming. This must be a nightmare.

I had thoroughly executed Bob's advice, a good thing for my passenger and me, but not for the 170. After it sank out of sight, I began to swim in the direction where I had last seen the *sáhila*. The rain was intense, and I kept repeating in my head: This has to be a bad dream. It cannot be happening to me.

I seemed to be swimming aimlessly, but I finally felt the sandy bottom with the palms of my hands. I tried to stand up but I couldn't so I crawled to shore on my hands and knees. Then I heard a female voice: "Are you all right? Are you okay?"

I looked up and saw a striking female, dressed in cut-off shorts and a T-shirt with a white dove printed on her chest. She helped me stand, and I felt for sure I was hallucinating. I thought, Christ! This is real. I must have died and I'm in heaven. Holy crap!

Just as the rain had started, it suddenly stopped. The sky cleared up and the sun shone brightly. Meanwhile a crowd had gathered around, and the savior that had found me clarified that she was an Australian nurse working as a volunteer in the island hospital. She offered me to go to the hospital for a checkup, but I refused, probably because

I didn't believe what had just happened or maybe because I was too embarrassed. Instead I sat on the stump of a palm tree to gather my thoughts and decide how I could recover my plane. As the 170's cargo of live lobsters was trapped at the bottom of the sea, the fishermen quickly organized the entire community in an attempt to recover their catch. In a matter of minutes they collected pieces of rope or cable, or whatever could work in making a long line. They sent one of the divers to tie the end of the rope to the tail wheel of the plane, which had settled at a depth of about 20 feet, and the village crowd began a rhythmic pull.

"*Guensak, bo, ba!*" One, two, three, shouted the director of the salvage operation and the enthusiastic crowd pulled in unison. I watched in disbelief at the tenacity of the islanders. I thought to myself, they'll never be able to pull out that 2,000 pound plane full of water and more than 300 pounds of lobsters.

But to my surprise, inch-by-inch I could see progress, and in about three hours they managed to get the plane on the beach. They distributed the lobsters among the owners and disappeared without a single word. It wasn't even eleven o'clock in the morning. I sat alone with my wrecked airplane, without the slightest idea of what to do. No idea whatsoever. There was really nothing I could do but wait for one of Paitilla's bush planes to give me a ride back to Panama City. I took out the radios and removed some instruments on the plane to take them to Panama, but that didn't take more than an hour. I never left the 170's side. I don't know if it was solidarity or guilt for what had happened.

At about five o'clock that afternoon I heard an airplane engine approaching. I raised the white flag on the bamboo pole next to the runway as a sign to pilots flying in the area that there're passengers on the ground. In a few minutes a twin-engine Islander piloted by Victor Yard landed. Victor listened attentively as I told him what had happened, and at the end of my story he solemnly stated that I wasn't the first to have this kind of accident, nor would I be the last. The difference though was that not everyone could tell the story. I don't know if that reassured or anguished me. On the trip back, I sat in silence analyzing what had happened and why it had happened. I had learned a great lesson and though I was unharmed, it had come at a great cost, not only to my ego. I had lost my airplane.

Among pilots, there are levels of comfort plateaus, each reached through routine and practice. This, if not held in check, sooner or later reaches its limit. As we become comfortable in one plateau, we either move on to a higher level or stay where we are. Obviously I was comfortable in that plateau and in my mind, I evaluated the risk factor as medium. On that flight, that sense of comfort bit me in the ass. And bit me hard.

Above: The 170 parked on the Gamboa runway alongside the Panama Canal.

Below: Cloud Seeding Project pilots: Jake, Ibu, Kevin, Sally and Jim. Paitilla, Panama, 1983.

Above: Tam Syme, Andrea, Teo and Pat with the Thrush Commander S-2R during a visit to Changuinola, Panama. 1977.

Below: Pat with the 170 in Coronado, Panama.

Above: The 170 after the splashdown. Nargana, San Blas, Panama. 1978.

Part 5
The Remarkable 180

18 Rebirth of a Classic
19 The Yellow Fever
20 Flight of Uncertainty
21 Vital Oxygen
22 Possessed by the Devil
23 Farewell to a Friend

Chapter 18
Rebirth of a Classic

A few days after the accident in Nargana, I rented a plane and flew with Bob to the island. Since the 170 hadn't suffered major structural damage and only the tail elevators had been bent in the salvage operation, Bob assured me that it was a matter of straightening the elevators, rinsing the engine with diesel oil, replacing the gasoline, clean the spark plugs and magnetos and that was it. Once the engine started, the rest was only to ferry fly it back to Paitilla. Well, it wasn't quite as easy as that. The few days that the 170 had sat in the open air were enough to guarantee that it wouldn't fly. We did what was supposed to be done to start it and came up with nothing. We cranked the engine until we almost exhausted the rented plane's battery, but it just wouldn't start. We returned to Paitilla beaten and exhausted just as the sun was setting. I realized then that Bob had obviously not taken into consideration the salinity of the Caribbean Sea compared to a Canadian fresh water lake. I'm so glad now it ended up like that, because who knows how many of the engine's other vital components had been affected by the salt water that would have gone undetected until we were flying. We? I mean me flying, because Bob would have been flying the rented plane on that return trip. What a crappy deal that would have been!

Since my job in the Canal didn't allow me to take unjustified leave for so many days, I hired Sabin Castillo, a Paitilla mechanic to go to Nargana to disassemble the 170 and accompany it in a coastal motor launch that plied the coast between Colon and Cartagena, Colombia. Once the boat arrived at Colon, we loaded the plane on a boat trailer and brought it to Gamboa, where we backed up the whole airplane and trailer into Gatun Lake to wash off the salt water.

Although Bob insisted that restoring the plane back to flying conditions wouldn't be a big deal, I was skeptical about that prospect, since I found him overly cavalier when it came to fixing broken airplanes. The engine would have to be completely overhauled, the instruments replaced, as well as communication and navigational radios, in addition to treating the aluminum skin that had been exposed to salt water, all of it, and repairing the parts affected during the retrieval from the bottom of the ocean. Although the aircraft's hull was insured, the repair would cost much more than what I would get from the claim. Besides, I didn't have time to dedicate myself to such a project and resigned myself to just accept the loss of the plane.

In Paitilla airport there were a number of non-flying airplanes at the far end of the runway that had been abandoned for one reason or another. Among those, there was a 1955 Cessna 180 sans motor, propeller and instruments or radios; in other words, it had been cannibalized. HP-341. I found out the owner was Ladislao Sosa and that the engine was in a shop in Miami, Florida, awaiting funds for an overhaul. We came to an agreement and soon I was the owner of that battered-looking airplane. Though I had never flown one, I knew the reputation of the Cessna 180 as a can-do airplane. Bob offered his help and know-how to restore the airplane in exchange for the recently wrecked 170 and the fuselage of another 170 that I had bought from Alex Stettmeier after it had suffered a mishap while taking off from Plaza de Caisan in Renacimiento, Chiriqui.

For these two disassembled airplanes, Bob would rescue the 180's engine from the Miami shop and take it to Canada for a major overhaul. The problem of the missing propeller was solved once I bought a time-expired propeller from Mike Petrosky that he had stored in the Aviones de Panama depot. It would have to be sent to an authorized shop in the US for overhaul, but that was within my budget based on the insurance money from the 170. I took the propeller as personal baggage on a commercial flight to New Orleans and hand delivered it to an authorized propeller shop there. In a matter of weeks I received an as-new certified propeller.

With the help of enthusiastic friends and family, we removed the various layers of paint off the wings, empennage and the fuselage, treated them accordingly with chemicals and Bob took care of the painting, while May, Bob's wife, upholstered the seats. The paint color chosen was a bright caterpillar yellow, which earned the 180 its nickname "Fiebre Amarilla" (Yellow Fever). A few months later, after Bob and family left, I received the overhauled engine from Canada accompanied with all the required paperwork and with the help of the instrument technician, Manuel Fletcher; the radio technician, Wilbur Morrison; the local sheet metal specialist, Alexander Luison; and with Tato's guidance, I ended up with a like-new 180. Years before, while the plane was operated by Servicos Aereos del Canajagua Azul, a rear baggage door, a third set of side windows, and a bench seat in the cargo compartment to accommodate two additional persons for a total of six had been installed. Just the same as the latest factory model 180's. A beautiful sight!

As I've mentioned before, I don't like to carry passengers on test flights, but on that first flight, Jose Salvador Pepe Muñoz, who owned and flew a 180, insisted on accompanying me, and I agreed. Brave soul. Everything worked perfectly and I knew I had one of the best single-engine airplanes ever built. It was not a DC-3, but it was the next best thing, a Cessna 180. Little did I know what a tremendous plane it would turn out to be!

My connection with the 180s had begun when our Changuinola neighbor Luis Flores flew my mother, my newborn son Teo and me, in his 180 from Almirante to David crossing the Cordillera late one afternoon. The need to have access to a working incubator motivated that trip. That one fact, as well as many other technical reasons I was to find out later, had made me a loyal follower of the Cessna 180. I still am.

Chapter 19
The Yellow Fever

As a family we had a number of unique experiences traveling in the Yellow Fever through Central America, Mexico and the US. In Mexico we visited the Mixtla and Monte Alban archaeological sites of the Zacateca pre-Columbian culture that date beyond 500 BC in Oaxaca; we toured the site of Wilbur and Orville Wright's first flight in Kitty Hawk, North Carolina; the Smithsonian Aviation Museum in Washington, DC; and met hospitable people in the small towns up and down that route who made our stay enjoyable. It could more accurately be described as a flying vacation.

On that first trip across the North American continent, it is also worth mentioning an experience with the Mexican and US immigration authorities, which for me was a lesson in how, despite pre-conceived assumptions, understanding and goodwill can open doors. We were leaving Mexico from the Matamoros airport. The Mexican authorities had stamped our passports with the date and time of exit, and we were good to go. After our farewells, we flew about seven minutes, crossed the Rio Grande and landed in Brownsville, Texas, the US port of entry. The US immigration agent, a young Mex-Texan, saw that my passport didn't have a US visa, so he directed us to fly back to Mexico. I tried my best to explain to him that I had left my old expired passport that contained a US visa in Panama and that since the plane had already left Mexico, I would be in trouble trying to re-enter because I didn't have the required re-entry permit. I asked for permission for the plane to remain on the ramp while I crossed the border back into Mexico to obtain a visa to enter the US. But he wouldn't budge no matter how much I tried to reason with him. He said my family could enter since they were US citizens, but I had to leave, together with the airplane since it couldn't remain parked on the ramp, and no, I couldn't refuel. He kept repeating this over and over. With no other alternative, we all walked back and got in the plane and flew back to Matamoros, where only moments before we had left. The same Mexican immigration officer who had stamped our passports when we exited the country was there to receive us.

"*Órale, Comandante*. Don't tell me; let me guess. The *pinches gringos* at immigration won't let you in and now you need to get back into Mexico, but don't have an entry permit because you already left. Am I right?" he said with a twisted smile on his face.

"Well, yes," I answered meekly.

"*Sí, pues ándele*. Tomorrow we'll talk about your exit permits. *Tranquilo*."

I thanked him, and made a mental calculation of how much this favor would cost me. I estimated it would come out to be no less than two hundred dollars. That's almost 100 gallons of fuel, or about 10 flight hours, or about 1,500 miles. That's a lot of hay! We found a hotel near the center of town and that night watched a World Cup soccer game, anticipating the hassle we would probably have to face in the morning. The next day, after a restless night, I was at the US consulate at 7 a.m. sharp, but the line was two blocks long. I decided to try to pull some influence as a US government employee with the Panama Canal, and walked to the head of the line and showed my Federal Employee ID card to the security guard. Right away I was led to the front of the line and half an hour later I had my US visa. Things are looking up, I remember thinking.

After an enjoyable no-rush breakfast, we arrived at the airport and went directly to immigration where the same agent from the previous day met us: "Well then, Commander, do you already have your papers in order for the *gringo migra*?"

"*Todo en orden, caballero*," I answered, waiting for the inevitable bribe request.

"*Ah, bueno. Vaya con Dios,*" he said as he offered me his hand to shake, not to receive any money.

I was taken aback for a moment but seeing that there was no intention on his part for a handout, I shook his hand and waved as we headed to the plane. Approaching Brownsville airport we were number two behind a Mexican Cessna 206. Once on the ground and entering the terminal to the immigration counter, we heard the Mexican 206 pilot explaining to the immigration agent, a different one from the day before, that he had forgotten his passport, personal identification documents, driver's license, ID, pilot's license, everything, in his car in Veracruz. He only had a copy of his flight plan. He said the purpose of the trip was to pick up spare parts for a tractor. The immigration agent, who looked like he was right out of a western movie with his revolver strapped to his belt, stared at the pilot for a moment and then said: "Okay, go to that phone and call for them to bring the parts to the airport while you sit in the lounge and wait."

What I had just witnessed was how a person in a fix had been given a practical and reasonable solution to his problem. When it was our turn, I narrated what had taken place with us the previous day with the other agent. The man just shook his head and said, "Ah, he was just trying to demonstrate his power. Foolish young whippersnapper, there was no need for that."

Who would have believed it? The one person one would think would give you a hand based on cultural homogeneity didn't, and one from whom you would least expect it, did. By prejudging appearances and stereotypes, I had erred miserably, but I learned my lesson well.

The 180 provided countless experiences for us as a family: Camping under the wing on San Jose Island or in a pasture during the Las Tablas carnivals, or routine trips to both the Caribbean and Pacific beaches come to mind. You could pack four adults, baggage and five hours of fuel on board and not have a doubt of the airplane's performance. It was a working airplane and a reliable family transport.

Chapter 20
Flight of Uncertainty

One Friday night, on April 28, 1984, my friend Eddie phoned to ask me to replace him on a flight the next day. He wasn't going to be able to comply. Eddie Armbruster, an instructor and mentor, had helped me in obtaining my private and commercial FAA licenses as well as my instrument and instructor ratings. I was indebted. Eddie regularly flew members of his church on social assistance missions to the Kuna, Embera and Wounan communities in San Blas and Darien.

"Sure I can, just give me the details," I answered, assuming that the passengers were Mormon missionaries.

At the airport that Saturday morning, waiting next to my 180, this person walks up to me and identifies himself as Mark and tells me the flight we're going on is a reconnaissance flight over the Pedasi area on the Azuero peninsula where his company is planning to build a dock to serve tuna fishing boats. Oh well, so much for the Mormon missionaries.

We took off and while still climbing to our final altitude heading westerly to the Azuero peninsula, Mark transmits over the intercom that we need to land at Chame airport to pick up his colleague. No problem, it's on the route. We land and pick up Glenn, who after takeoff informs me of a change of plans. Instead of the Azuero peninsula, we're to fly over the Darien coastline. In those days there had been several kidnapping cases of Paitilla-based planes that were never heard of again, but the rumors abounded of who perpetuated them: the Colombian guerrilla forces, the FARC

(Fuerzas Armadas Revolucionarias de Colombia). These two strangers on board were obviously not Colombians, but then again, who could guarantee they weren't up to some shady business?

"The Darien coast is more than 150 miles long," I reply. "Where exactly do you want to go?"

"We're looking for locations where we can build a wharf, upstream of the mouth of a river," Glenn answered.

"Okay," I said and veered eastward, heading to the mouth of the Maje River.

Then one of them says more specifically, "Actually, we're interested in the rivers beyond La Palma."

This is odd, I thought. Why not tell me exactly where they want to go?

At every river mouth we'd come upon, we'd fly inland at an altitude of about 500 feet. We'd been flying for more than two hours when we entered the Sambu River. This part of Darien was familiar to me. I had landed several times in Boca de Sabalo, on the banks of the Sambu River, but that day we flew further upriver. There the jungle becomes thicker and the ground begins to rise towards the Colombian border. By this time, black clouds had begun to form to the east, towards where we were heading.

The only mode of transportation this far upriver is by canoe. I kept wondering what the hell it was that these two were looking for?

Feeling uncomfortable about the situation, I said to them, "This is as far as we go. The weather's beginning to look ugly and we only have two and a half hours of fuel for the two-hour return flight."

Both insisted we continue a few more miles, and though I exaggerated a bit, I held my ground and simply turned and headed for home. I knew that they hadn't liked my decision, but I didn't care. The hell with them!

We returned to Paitilla in silence and when we landed Glenn asked how much was owed for the flight.

"The gasoline for four hours of flight is one hundred dollars."

Glenn, who seemed to be the boss, put a wad of bills in my hand and said, "Here's two hundred. No receipts."

A few days later, on Tuesday, the headlines on the front page of *La Prensa* reported that the Panama Defense Forces (FFDD) had discovered a cocaine-processing laboratory in Darien, upstream of the Sambu River, in the foothills of the Serrania del Sapo mountain range and had made arrests. They had supposedly confiscated a French-made turbine Alouette helicopter; several assault weapons, and an RPG (Rocket Propelled Grenade) launcher.

Shit, that's where we were on that last reconnaissance flight. I confronted Eddie about this headline news only to find out that these passengers he had entrusted to me were actually US Embassy officials. Eddie rolled with laughter as he filled me in, claiming that he didn't know the purpose of the flight beforehand. After that episode I was so upset with Eddie that I swore I'd never fly for him again, but I knew deep down inside, that eventually I'd forget about it. After all, Eddie was a good friend and wasn't it a way of logging hours anyway?

A week later, another story broke in the media that a FFDD colonel had been arrested and was accused of being involved with the laboratory, but rumor had it that the colonel was nothing more than a scapegoat. He was in jail for a year before being released, but that's another story for someone else to tell. Actually, my passengers on that day were DEA agents that had information about the existence of a cocaine-processing laboratory somewhere about 10 miles from the mouth of a river in Darien. When they didn't find the exact location on that flight with me that day, supposedly they had given the FFDD an ultimatum to do something, or the information would be filtered to the press that there was a cocaine-processing laboratory operating in Panamanian territory under the authorities' noses. At that, the FFDD took action. This story I found out thirty years later from the person I was buying a Cessna 170 from and who had been CIA chief in Panama in those days.

I've often wondered what would have happened if I hadn't stuck to my decision to turn around and head home. What if those guarding the lab had fired their RPG at us? We would've been declared missing on a flight over the Darien jungle. Period. *Coño!* In cases like this, being a stubborn intransigent hard-ass definitely pays off.

Chapter 21
Vital Oxygen

On a flight from David to Panama with my sister Nan as a passenger, I experienced a situation that definitely ingrained in me the importance of being prepared for possible unplanned scenarios. The flight was in March, that time of year when cloud clusters begin to form in the afternoons parallel to the mountain range and make for an uncomfortable ride if you ply through them or under them. I wanted to make the flight as pleasant as possible for Nan by climbing over the cumulus clouds to avoid the turbulence. I submitted my visual flight plan for 9,500 feet, but as we reached that altitude, I realized that I would have to climb even more because the cumulus clouds were maturing into cumulonimbus, the big boys. I notified the Malek Airport tower that I was ascending to 13,500 feet, aware that after thirty minutes in excess of 12,000 feet of altitude; one is exposed to hypoxia. Although I was conscious of the circumstances, I estimated that it wouldn't take long to over fly that cloud formation. My sister was asleep in the seat next to me, most likely due to the effects of the altitude, so I decided to exercise my mind by doing mathematical calculations and reciting mentally well-known verses. Staying mentally alert is a way to temporarily postpone hypoxia.

I don't know how much time elapsed, but the next thing I remember was hearing a voice in my headset calling out: "Hotel Papa 341, Hotel Papa 341, what are your intentions? Do you copy?" It was the Panama Control Center located in Ancon, Balboa, who was trying to contact me. I replied that I copied them and that my final destination was Paitilla.

"Well, be aware you are flying due north over the Veraguas coast. Turn immediately to a 180° heading and begin a descent to 10,000 feet in visual conditions," the Center advised.

Obviously they had seen the airplane stray off its intended route on the radar. How had I gotten so far off route? The only logical explanation is that the hypoxia had begun to take effect on me. If I had heard the Center calling me and was able to react accordingly, it meant that the total effects of hypoxia hadn't yet taken over. When that happens, the pilot experiences a total blackout.

That flight was on a Sunday, and the very next day I acquired a portable oxygen bottle to ensure that I would not be caught in a similar situation in the future. Years later on a family trip from Panama to the US, while crossing the Sierra Madre in Mexico between Oaxaca and Veracruz, we had to climb to 15,500 feet, and even though it was for no more than fifteen minutes, I had my oxygen mask on as soon as we passed 12,000 feet. That supplemental oxygen bottle was on board on any flight I took, whether it was of short or long duration at any planned altitude. Another lesson well learned.

Chapter 22
Possessed by the Devil

For a while I utilized the 180 for skydiving operations on the Calzada Larga runway, adjacent to Lake Alhajuela. On Saturdays and Sundays, skydiving enthusiasts from Panama and Canal Zone clubs gathered and made an outing of skydiving. The 180 was ideal for parachuting because it could accommodate up to four jumpers with their heavy equipment and quickly climb to the selected altitude, which made it an efficient airplane for skydiving operations.

One Sunday, when I was on my last flight, I loaded the 180 with three U.S. Army club skydivers. Two of them were regulars, but the third was not. He was a big, heavy-set guy, unlike the mean and lean typical skydivers I'd come across. I calculated his weight at 240 pounds, plus the weight of two parachutes, the main and the auxiliary. Because of his bulk, he had problems accommodating himself inside the cabin. I noticed he seemed more apprehensive and not as relaxed as the other two who were joking around as we climbed to 9,000 feet. The first two jumped, and as I patted the third on his helmet to indicate we were over the target, he motioned with hand signals to circle once again. I figured he wasn't sure of our position over the target, so I complied and circled. It took me a couple of minutes to turn 360° and position the plane again over the target. He jumped. I watched waiting for him to open his chute before initiating my spiral descent. I saw that his parachute was deployed but not opened. Then suddenly, around 7,000 feet, I saw him deploy the reserve chute without first getting rid of the main one.

Shit! I couldn't believe what was happening. I knew from being among skydivers that that was a definite no-no. In the event of an emergency when the main chute doesn't open, it must be released before opening the auxiliary chute to prevent them from getting tangled up. And that's what happened. The two chutes got entangled and he was descending in a fast spiral. He hit the ground just off the runway edge, but from the air I could see that the impact had made a depression in the ground. When I landed, his lifeless body was already being loaded in a car to take him to the nearest hospital. I later learned that he had been washed out as a candidate of a US Special Forces High Altitude/Low Opening (HALO) military specialty. The reason was supposedly for lack of resolve or character. I can't recall the exact terminology. If so, why would he want to continue jumping out of perfectly operating airplanes? Maybe it was a need to prove to himself that he did have that determination?

After that fatal accident, members of the Military and Canal Zone clubs were forbidden to participate in skydiving until an investigation of why the accident occurred was concluded, but the Panamanian clubs kept the activity same as usual. Two weeks after the accident, another accident occurred for the same reason: Not releasing the main chute before opening the reserve chute. And to top it off, it happened in my 180 and with me as a pilot. What was going on? This particular skydiver barely weighed 120 pounds. He was a member of Shorty Miranda's club. Shorty was a veteran skydiving instructor. In this accident the skydiver impacted the asphalt smack in the middle of the runway, but miraculously he survived. I quickly landed next to him, and the other skydivers loaded him in the 180, and I flew him immediately to Paitilla where an ambulance was waiting to take him to the hospital. The next day I was informed that he had broken both legs, but apart from that, he was fine. Scared out of his wits, I imagine, but fine.

That same Monday, Lotty Cruz, who was like the parachuting coordinator or grand marshal in Calzada Larga, called me.

"Ibu, I'd like to meet with you this afternoon to talk about something important," he said.

"Sure, Lotty. I can be on the El Piloto terrace at the airport at 4:30. See you there," I answered wondering what he wanted on such short notice.

Lotty showed up accompanied by Shorty just a few minutes after I had arrived.

"Well, what's going on?" I said after greeting them.

Lotty begins, "Ibu, you know that the two accidents we've had have been from your airplane and after consulting the matter with Father Karamañitis from the San Miguelito parish, he strongly advises that he perform an exorcism on your plane to scare away the evil spirits that apparently accompany it."

I gaze first at Lotty then at Shorty.

"Look, Lotty, both you and Shorty, like all the other skydivers, know very well what caused those two accidents and it has nothing, I repeat, nothing to do with my airplane. It's simply either a lack of good instruction, or a lack of balls by those two individuals; and if the reason is the lack of balls, then they shouldn't have been jumping out of airplanes. So, here's my answer. No! Go find something else to blame, but leave my airplane out of this." I got up and left.

As a result of the accidents, the parachuting activity decreased for a while, but it took hold again not long after because skydiving, like flying, is an urge that's not easy to push aside. For some reason or another, I didn't fly jumpers again, but whether or not Fr. Karamañitis's analysis was correct, I have no idea.

Chapter 23
Farewell to a Friend

During the US invasion of Panama on December 20, 1989, the 180 was shot up, as were many other airplanes in Paitilla. Several bullets pierced its tail, wings and part of the fuselage. I contracted Antonio Nica Velasquez, a sheet metal repairman, to repair the fuselage damage and to rebuild both wings, the section most affected, to optimal conditions. Every afternoon I would stop by his shop to watch him work. It took some months before the 180 was ready to fly. A few days later, I was asked to fly a portable water purification plant to Bocas after the earthquake had caused major damage to the island. It was a good opportunity to test-fly the airplane to check for necessary rigging in cruise flight and control response, as well as for airspeed. Though I didn't think about it at the time, this would actually be a test flight after a major repair. At the last minute, I invited fellow pilot and 180 enthusiast, Billy Earle, to accompany me on that flight. The airplane flew straight and level and was responsive to the inputs and flew as fast as ever. It had been a good restoration. On the return trip, I gave up my left seat to Billy so he could fly the hour and a half trip back to Paitilla. As we were abeam Escudo de Veraguas Island, and as those who have flown that route know, we encountered the usual foul weather. There was nothing else to do but to go right through it. Although the wings were rocking up and down in the strong turbulence, I was relaxed because I knew that Nica had done an excellent repair job. As I looked over at Billy, concentrated on flying, it hit me that I hadn't mentioned that this was the 180's first flight after being shot up. He was so engrossed in flying that I decided not to tell him.

I didn't realize it then, but that would be the last flight I would make in the 180. The engine and prop were due for a major overhaul, an expense I couldn't justify, so with a heavy heart and much regret, I decided to sell it to a Colombian buyer.

The transaction for the sale took place in his hotel room where I received the equivalent of sixteen thousand dollars in twenty-dollar bills. That's a lot of bills. This wasn't a normal manner to exchange money, but naïve, unthinking me; I left the hotel with two large shopping bags full of grimy dirty bills. The next day when I went to the bank to make a deposit, the bank officials stringently scrutinized me. They wanted to know where the money had come from, and I had to provide affidavits to justify that amount of cash. I thought money laundering was something involving millions of dollars, not a small amount like what I had sold my 180 for.

The ferry pilot who came from Colombia to fly the 180 back hadn't been in an airplane for years. He was a retired crop duster, so he said, and had lots of trouble taking off and landing the airplane when I was checking him out. I cringed when I saw him take off for Colombia with my cherished 180. A few months later, I learned it had been wrecked, but knowing Colombian diligence, I'm sure that it's been repaired and that it's flying in the savannahs of Caqueta. Great plane that HP-341. To this day I regret that sale.

Above 1: The 180 in El Hato de Volcan, Chiriqui, Panama.

Above 2: The 180 in Santiago, Veraguas, Panama.

Above 3: The 180 over El Valle del Madroño on the way to the coast of San Blas.

Above: Ibu at home in the 180.
Below: Arrival at Pavas airport, Costa Rica, on the way to the US in the Yellow Fever, 1982.

Right Above: On final, La Enea runway, Los Santos, Panama.
Right Center: Instructor Shorty Miranda briefing his students before boarding the 180, Calzada Larga, 1987.
Right Below: Ricardo Sierra, Manuelito Alvarado and Ibu next to the 180 at a fly-in in Chame.

The Remarkable 180 153

Part 6
The Maule

24 The Reluctant Missionary
25 Rescued
26 A Prolonged Restoration
27 In the Air Again
28 Erratic Behavior
29 Hindered
30 Back on Track
31 Energized Plane and Pilot
32 Duty Fulfilled

Chapter 24
The Reluctant Missionary

Doctor Gruber, a US missionary doctor serving the Kuna ethnic community in San Blas, was based on the island of Ustupo. To say he was an interesting character is an understatement. He was highly appreciated for his dedication that was recognized not only in Panama, but also abroad. He flew his Piper Super Cub PA-18 weekly to Paitilla to stock up on supplies for the island clinic and his family. The Super Cub, manufactured until 1949, was and still is a popular aircraft, especially in back country areas because of its superiority in terms of takeoff and landings on short and improvised strips. With a structure made up of metal tubes covered in cloth and a 150 horsepower engine, the Super Cub makes for an excellent weight hauling bush plane. However, seeing this particular Super Cub didn't inspire much confidence at all mainly because parts of the fuselage and wings were patched with a tape commonly known as 100 mph tape, which could be obtained from the USAF shops on Howard AFB. Dr. Gruber wasn't necessarily a reckless pilot, though a bit too daring, and it wasn't unusual to see him land with three passengers in the back single-passenger seat, exceeding the limit of people designated for the Super Cub. He must have known what the Super Cub could and couldn't do. He had lots of hours flying it.

One afternoon he landed, got out and with his characteristic wide-brimmed Panama hat, greeted everyone he came across. His mission that day was to pick up two members of the church he belonged to in the US and who apparently financially supported the mission in Ustupo. At a glance, you could see that the passengers were not featherweights like the Kuna passengers he normally transported. And what's more, with their backpacks it was obvious that the takeoff would be with an overweight plane. Dr. Gruber didn't flinch and could be heard assuring them that everything was under control. He managed to squeeze the two passengers in the back seat and forced the backpacks under and behind the backbench seat. He left the heavier luggage in the Tatsa offices to be flown to Ustupo the next day.

The takeoff would be towards the north, against the prevailing wind, towards the trees. The length of the Paitilla runway even in those days was more than enough for a normally loaded Super Cub, but this time the weight on board was way more than normal. Far off at the other end of the runway, we watched as he began his takeoff run. As the Super Cub approached, the tail wheel was still on the ground and just as he rolled beyond the midway point, he cut engine power; he aborted the takeoff almost in front of the airport terminal where we all were standing. As he taxied back and got off the plane, he started to remove the backpacks making it obvious his intention was to lighten the plane, convinced that was the reason the Super Cub couldn't get the necessary takeoff speed. His two passengers, visibly shaken, got out of the plane and refused to be part of a new attempt, and there was no way that Dr. Gruber could convince them otherwise. Eventually, Tatsa acceded to transport the visitors that afternoon while Dr. Gruber would fly alone with the backpacks. Unknowingly, that flight would cause a significant upgrade for Dr. Gruber.

In the months after that incident, a Maule Lunar Rocket M-5 arrived at Paitilla straight from the factory in

Moultrie, Georgia. It was equipped with a 210 horsepower fuel injection engine and the latest technology in communication and navigation radios onboard. This single engine, four-seat STOL taildragger airplane was for Dr. Gruber. The ferry pilot didn't know where to contact Dr. Gruber, so I offered my services as liaison and interpreter for him. This was a donation that the doctor knew nothing about. From the Tatsa offices where they had an HF communications radio I sent a message to Dr. Gruber that he was needed in Paitilla to receive a recently arrived shipment. Eventually, we found out this gesture or donation was at the suggestion of the visitors who months before had experienced that hairy takeoff attempt in the vintage Super Cub. The Maule was for the missionary doctor's use. The Super Cub was to be replaced. For Dr. Gruber, flying the Maule would not be a problem since he was an accomplished taildragger pilot.

What the donors didn't know was that Dr. Gruber had already made plans to leave for the US to specialize in microscopic neurosurgery. This being the case, he sold the Maule, with less than fifty hours of use, to Reverend James Thomas of the Union Church of Balboa. Reverend Thomas was a tricycle pilot, a nose wheel pilot, and had no experience in taildraggers. He promptly approached me to give him lessons to enable him to fly the Maule. I hadn't flown a Maule before, but since it was a tail wheel airplane, after consulting with local more experienced taildragger pilots, they assured me that there would be no problem, so I agreed to the Reverend's request. By then, I had recently obtained my FAA flight instructor license, and the Reverend would be my first taildragger student.

We agreed that we would fly out of Gamboa Airport in the afternoons after work. The Reverend, over twice my age, although disciplined, was somewhat hardheaded. After about thirteen hours of difficult instruction, I soloed him in Calzada Larga, which had a 4,000-foot long concrete runway. When we arrived back at Gamboa, I then checked him out on that grass strip, which was long enough and safe for a beginner. When I signed his logbook authorizing him to fly solo, I emphasized that it was only for operations in the Calzada Larga and Gamboa runways, until he felt comfortable with the plane. Then, I would work with him on short unimproved runways such as those found in the San Blas islands, knowing of his intentions to expand his mission there.

The very next day I learned that the Maule had been wrecked in Aligandi, San Blas, where the runway consisted of a narrow 1,100-foot gravel strip, and that the pilot was the Reverend. What was the Reverend doing in Aligandi? My instructions had been clear and precise: Calzada Larga and Gamboa only. From one day to the next, he couldn't have flown enough hours in that airplane to be able to fully handle it comfortably. I had figured it would take him at least another five hours landing and taking off on familiar long, hard-surfaced runways until he completely dominated the plane. I had misjudged him.

A few days later, he told me the full story himself. That day, he had made two attempts to land in Aligandi, but since the wind was crossed, he had to miss both approaches. He made up his mind by the third attempt that he was going to land no matter what. He did, but unfortunately the Maule went off the sandy track and nosed over. Neither he nor his passenger was hurt, nor was his valuable load of eggs and cases of cooking oil lost. It's not easy to control what students who own their airplanes might do. I should know. I had been one.

After a few days, the insurance company contacted me to assist them in determining whether the Maule was a total loss or could be repaired. So I flew to Aligandi with a mechanic and we evaluated the damages and determined that it was repairable, but that it would have to be disassembled and transported by sea to the port of Colon and then by road to Paitilla where the shops that could do the work were located. The engine had had a sudden stop so it would have to be sent to the US for its major overhaul; the bent propeller would have to be replaced; the battered and twisted wings would have to be repaired, as would the tubular landing gear. The logistics of bringing the plane would be the most crucial part of the repair, as it required a lot of improvisation. The insurance company had no interest in these matters and proposed to sell me the Maule where and how it was for the sum of six thousand dollars. I calculated that the repairs and replacements would end up costing twenty thousand dollars. The Blue Book value of that repaired plane, with less than sixty hours of flight time, would be between fifty thousand and sixty thousand. I saw the project as an opportunity to provide me enough earnings to cover the multi-engine and instrument licenses that I lacked. I went back to the bank for a loan and soon got it approved. They knew me by now.

And that's how I became the owner of a wrecked Maule in the middle of the Kuna Reserve. That was the easy part. Now came the difficult task of getting the airplane back to Paitilla.

Chapter 25
Rescued

A month after the Maule wreck, I returned to Aligandi with Brian, the son of my friend and boss in the PCC, Frank Robinson. I had decided to disassemble the Maule with Brian's help to transport it by boat to Colon, and from there, to trailer it back to Gamboa by road. I hadn't the slightest idea of what I was getting into. The airstrip at Aligandi was on the mainland but the town itself was on the island by the same name, about a half-mile away. The plan was that Brian and I would camp on the runway next to the wreck and take full advantage of the daylight hours. We had already set up our lean-to and cots next to the runway strip when the village *sáhila* approached in a *cayuco*. He was accompanied by a group of islanders and had come to inquire about our purpose in their dominion. After carefully listening to my intention of hiring two assistants and to pay them each ten dollars a day, the *sáhila* objected vehemently. He said that instead of paying two assistants a total of twenty dollars a day, we were to pay four assistants five dollars each, and he would rotate the crews daily. That determination, he explained as he took me aside, was to maintain the established pay system for daily labor and at the same time, spread the wealth among the community. That made sense to me, especially knowing the Kuna's cooperative work habits. That same afternoon we up-turned the airplane and set it on what was left of the landing gear. The removal of the propeller, wings, struts and horizontal stabilizer was left for the next day. The engine, landing gear, vertical stabilizer and rudder would remain on the fuselage for easier mobilization. I had already removed the flight instruments and radios during my inspection visit for the insurance company.

The *sáhila* had also let us know that under no uncertain terms could we camp there on the mainland. We had to stay at the Aligandi Hotel. Once on the island and accommodated at the hotel, the manager, Pedro Martinez showed up to welcome us. He proudly informed us that he had been a cook at the Ft. Kobbe military base barracks, and assured us he was a versatile chef, as he referred to himself. That evening, over a dinner of fresh stewed fish and rice and coconut accompanied with green fried plantains, we found out he was true to his word. It was spectacular. The breakfasts the next two days were also top of the line. We skipped lunch so as to not stop our work program, but this only increased our anticipation for the dinner that awaited us at the hotel: Lobsters, octopus or sautéed fish?

On the second day, once the Maule was disassembled, the challenge was to get the fuselage and wings from the mainland to the pier on the island. The separation between the wheels of the landing gear was too wide to be able to place it on a single *cayuco*, and as we needed the landing gear to be attached to the fuselage in order to roll it, removing it was not an option. Brian and I discussed the matter among ourselves and consulted with our local assistants, and decided to use another *cayuco* and secure it with a 2x4 board at the bow of each *cayuco* to provide the necessary separation and thus accommodate each of the tires inside a *cayuco*. Another 2x4 was positioned on the sterns to tie and support the tail wheel, so that it wouldn't contact the salt water. What we hadn't considered was the winds that would act on the Maule's large tail surface making it respond like a sail and rendering the steering of our improvised floating transport impossible. Maybe even cause the whole contraption to overturn. That would really ruin our day. Perceiving our dilemma, one of the Kuna assistants proposed we wait until nightfall, which is when the wind subsides, to make the crossing to the island pier. At eight o'clock that night, with a rope tied to a third motorized *cayuco* towing us, we crossed our valuable cargo to the island. It seemed like the whole town was there to help us lift the fuselage and the wings six feet above the water and up onto the concrete pier. We went to bed exhausted but satisfied with the achievements, in large part due to the islanders' cooperation. They had made the occasion a festive one. The laughter and commotion were heard late into the night. At dawn, the coastal motorboat that was due from Capurgana, on the Caribbean coast of Colombia on its way to Colon, had already docked.

We strapped the Maule's parts onto the deck top, and embarked on what would be a continuation of an extended adventure: Eleven hours of diesel vapors and an unrelenting sun, without a doubt, was the worst part of this experience. When we saw the Colon docks on the horizon, we were filled with relief. We had completed the second stage of the project to get the Maule flying again. I was convinced that after this major effort, we'd get it to fly, no matter what. What I didn't realize at the time was that it would take seven years to achieve it.

Chapter 26
A Prolonged Restoration

After years of repairing and tracking down parts for the wrecked Maule, we were ready to start the assembly. The workplace was Alfred Chase's garage. Alfred and I had joined efforts to undertake the renovating of this airplane. By now, we both realized what a major task it would be. Every afternoon we dedicated three or four hours to the project. By having it totally disassembled, we were able to carefully inspect the whole airplane. Antonio the sheet metal guru was rebuilding the wings in Paitilla, but we didn't have anyone knowledgeable in restoring fabric-covered airplanes. That was a specialty that had been lost over time once aluminum became the preferred skin instead of fabric. The last technician had been Humberto Goldoni, one of the pioneers in aviation in Panama during the post Second World War years. Luckily for us, we met Trevor Zandor, who had arrived in Panama looking to buy abandoned airplanes. Trevor was both a pilot and restorer of old planes and knew the techniques of fabric covering airplanes, and most importantly, offered to help us do the job of covering, sewing, ironing, and doping prior to painting. He was our savior.

In a matter of days we had the whole fuselage covered and ready to be painted. For the repair of the landing gear we tapped on Leonardo Leo Stewart's knowledge in the art of specialized chrome molybdenum welding. Leo was well known in the aeronautical community and possessed several talents. He was continually called upon to repair air conditioning, pressurization, hydraulic, and aircraft fuel systems. He brought his argon welding equipment to the Los Rios garage, and he basically rebuilt a new landing gear using the bent and twisted original as a guide.

Now we were ready to trailer the fuselage to the airport for the final assembly. In Tato's shop, we mounted the repaired wings, overhauled engine and propeller. Then came adjusting the flight control and wiring the instruments and radios. The painting was done once the plane was re-assembled. The color chosen: Jet-black.

Once DAC's experts completed the inspection and approved the paperwork, it was time to test fly the Maule. Finally. I chose to be alone in that test flight, although there weren't many volunteers other than Al, but I declined his offer. I felt more comfortable being alone, probably so there could be no witness to see me peeing in my pants if something drastically went wrong. After two aborted takeoffs and the necessary adjustments to the engine and propeller controls, on the third attempt, it flew. But once on the ground again, we had to make further adjustments to the flight controls to get it to fly straight and level without pilot inputs. The black color with the red HP-705 registry numbers made the Maule look sinister. Rumor at Paitilla had it that that the black color was to go unnoticed during night flights. I neither denied nor affirmed that rumor, so the speculation grew, but it was simply painted black to break the standard.

Al had never flown taildraggers, so the first thing after that test flight was to check him out. We took advantage of those training flights and made a series of proving flights, and it was definitely a STOL airplane, but with a maximum of two people on board and restricted fuel. Under those conditions the Maule performed as the airplane operating manuals claimed. The takeoffs and climbs were impressive as were the short landings. We experimented operating in the Lagunas de Volcan runway, the highest one in Panama at 5,029 feet and the second highest, Cana, in Darien, at 1,327 feet with a steep grass gradient. During trials operating at maximum permissible takeoff weight using sand bags to increase the weight, it was marginal at best. Not fully loaded, the Maule could out climb the 180, but at gross weights, the 180 was a better performer.

These tests served to plan the next trip that would take me to high elevation strips flying through Central America and Mexico to the US. The Maule could carry 75 gallons of fuel for a seven-and-a-half hour range, but with four people on board plus baggage, takeoff weights needed to be restricted in high elevation airports. Anyway, flying in an airplane for longer than two hours without an onboard facility, can be agonizing for most bladders.

After flying 50 hours all over Panama without detecting any major problems, the Maule was ready for its flight to the US. The plan was for me to fly it up and once there, Al would then keep it there for a while before returning it to Panama.

Chapter 27
In the Air Again

During our stay in the US, I was scheduled to take my instrument flight check ride, so we decided to make it a family trip. Another flying adventure! We planned to spend the first night in San Jose, Costa Rica, and from there enter Mexico by way of Tapachula. From there our next programmed layovers would be Puerto Escondido and Guaymas, then cross the Gulf of California to Cabo San Lucas, Baja California. The trip would take in the best natural sites of the Mexican Pacific coast. It was our second trip of this nature as a family. The first had been in the 180 in 1982 up the Mexican Caribbean coast.

On the departure day, I had problems with the starter motor. It would barely turn the propeller. Tato, Isaac and Al, who were there to see us off, assumed it was the battery, and so did I. We lost precious hours while it was charging, but what bothered me the most was that I had flown the plane several hours the day before, and I was sure the electrical master switch had been turned off. So why was the battery not fully charged this morning? Around midday, with a fully charged battery, I tried again and the starter motor worked as expected, with lots of power. Instead of flying directly to Pavas airport in San Jose, I decided to make a technical stop in David to eliminate the possibility that the alternator was not charging the battery after starting the engine. When we landed, I took the plane to Ramon Gavilan, who had a repair shop on the premises. Gavilan checked and adjusted the wire connections and the ground wire. All was as it should be. I engaged the starter motor again and it started, but not with as much momentum as an hour and a half before when we had taken off from Paitilla. I evaluated the situation and decided to continue the flight on to Pavas, which was an hour and a half away. Although I ran the risk of running the battery down, the consequences weren't risky or dangerous.[27-A] I define it as a deliberately accepted risk.

Once in Pavas I would leave the Maule in Efrain Sanchez's shop. Many airplane owners and operators brought their airplanes from Panama to his shop to have work performed on them. The request I made to the shop foreman was to thoroughly examine the airplane's electrical system. The next day, the mechanics informed me that the plane was ready to go. Everything checked out as satisfactory. They had checked the alternator and starter and both were fine, but they suspected that the battery was not making good ground contact and therefore not charging efficiently, so they had added another cable to ground it better. I shouldn't have any more problems, and they had charged the battery. That diagnostic seemed reasonable to me, so we took off for Tapachula, with a technical stopover in San Salvador, El Salvador. In that first leg of that day, at 9,500 feet flying abeam the Nicaragua coast, I felt a slight vibration of the engine and I momentarily saw the engine drop 100-200 RPMs.

I checked the magnetos one by one and they were dropping within their normal range; I readjusted the engine fuel mixture according to the altitude, and everything was fine; I checked the propeller pitch and the manifold pressure gauges and both were where they should be. By then the engine was running normally again. After a fuel stop in San Salvador, and a rather sluggish start, we continued on to Tapachula where we spent the night and visited the sites of this interesting town. As a precaution I left the battery charging again, just in case. The next day the starter motor swung the prop just like it should. All was good, so we departed for Puerto Escondido.

The beaches at Puerto Escondido were everything we had anticipated; we were able to enjoy the waves and the warm waters of the Pacific without the hoards of tourists common in high season. The day we arrived, we were at the beach at sunset, relishing local beverages, Margaritas for me, and fruit smoothies for the kids all prepared under a thatched roof bar on the beach. At dawn the next day the saga began: Teo, Andrea and I woke up with upset stomachs. None of us had an appetite but the discomfort wasn't that bad as to cancel the next leg to Puerto Vallarta, our destination for that day. I decided to make a stopover in Acapulco to reevaluate the situation and determine if we should continue with the trip. It all depended on how our stomach ailments were developing. Five minutes after leveling off, I felt weak and asked Pat to take the controls. I told her to just to follow the coast until we reached Acapulco, an hour away. I felt drained so I closed my eyes and tried to recover my energy. After what seemed a short while, Pat woke me up. I had fallen asleep and we were already within sight of beautiful Acapulco. I took over the controls, contacted the tower and landed. As soon as I got off the plane, I knew I wasn't going to be able to continue the trip. The stomach spasms were more frequent and intense, both for me and for the kids, so we decided to stay in Acapulco until we felt better. Wise decision. The taxi driver we hired recommended the Hotel El Mirador, renowned for being the hotel where every room has a view of the famous cliff divers leaping from 136 feet into the waves breaking against the rocks. The truth is that no matter how bad I felt, the show was something spectacular, and for that brief moment I almost forgot my despicable condition. The next day we three woke up feeling so bad that we chose not to continue with the scheduled flight. The hotel management sent us a doctor who without hesitation diagnosed a virus but explained no more. He prescribed some medicine and ordered us to stay inactive, as if we could do something other than that. The third day, somewhat improved but still unable to taste a bite, we decided to continue to Puerto Vallarta. That night in Puerto Vallarta, using all my strength, we walked to a restaurant near the hotel to try to have dinner. Teo and Andrea had recovered in Acapulco, but I hadn't eaten for days. When the waiter saw my wasted face, he inquired if I had had drinks prepared with ice from some beach kiosk, so I recounted about the Margaritas and the fruit shakes prepared from shaved ice.

"Aha! That's it, that's where you went wrong," he said with an air of authority. "If the ice wasn't one of those cubes with a hole in the center, who knows where they got the water to make the ice."

"No, the ice was chopped," I answered.

"*Híjole*, that's the culprit. Sometimes even frogs appear frozen in those blocks of ice. Surely what you have is Moctezuma's Revenge.

I had heard of this sickness on previous trips through Mexico, but I had never fallen victim to it. I thought it was reserved for tourists from northern latitudes, not us *carnales* south of the Rio Grande. How wrong I was.

The waiter-turned-doctor insisted that what I needed was a steamed sea bass, without any condiments, not even salt, explaining the importance of trying to get the body to not reject the food. That way I could regain my strength. I followed his advice, and the next day after that insipid dinner, I woke up feeling like a new man.

Our next planned stop would be in Puerto Guaymas before crossing the Gulf of California to Cabo San Lucas, Baja California. But the days lost by the toxic Moctezuma's Revenge made us rethink our itinerary, and we decided to continue flying north and enter the US via Tucson, Arizona. Therefore, Los Mochis, Sinaloa, would be our next technical stop.

Chapter 28
Erratic Behavior

The flight from Puerto Vallarta to Guaymas, with a planned fuel stop in Los Mochis started out as non-eventful. Flying up the coastline I was able to enjoy the panorama for the first time in days. Once in Los Mochis airport, we ate lightly and drank only bottled water, following the Puerto Vallarta waiter's recommendations the night before.

With our flight plan stamped and approved, airport fees paid and the fuel tanks filled to fly five hours, we continued towards Guaymas in the state of Sonora. During our climb passing through 700 feet I felt the engine vibrate slightly and saw it was losing power. The RPMs had decreased enough to prevent the airplane from continuing to climb. Gradually we began to lose altitude. Shit! Now what?

Intuitively I turned on the electric fuel pump. I don't remember taking the time to determine that the engine wasn't getting enough fuel and that injecting gasoline through the electric pump, it would help recover the lost power. In this fuel injection engine, the electric pump is used exclusively to prime the motor before starting. As soon as the electric pump primed the lines, the engine picked up its lost RPMs. I breathed with relief. But I knew that the pump couldn't stay on for more than ten seconds. The high fuel pressure would flood the engine with too much fuel and cause it to stop. A rich cut, as it's known in aeronautical lingo.

With the recovered RPMs we continued to climb all

the while turning slowly to the right to return to the runway we had left behind. The sea was to the left, and I know from experience what it's like to have to ditch an airplane in the water. I chose to take my chances landing in the cane fields inland towards my right. I turned off the electric pump, and immediately the RPMs decreased and the engine shuddered, and we lost the few feet we had gained. I waited a few seconds before turning on the electric pump again and felt as the motor accelerated and we again ascended about 100 feet. By now, we were about 500 feet above the ground. The drill continued: pump on, we climbed; pump off, we descended. In what seemed like an eternity, I managed to align myself with the runway and land normally.

During all this time, which I estimate lasted between five to six minutes, no more, my three passengers never interrupted me to ask questions nor did they comment on what was happening. Not a peep. That behavior during those minutes of uncertainty, without a doubt, allowed me to concentrate and deal properly with the emergency. As soon as I had the opportunity on the ground, I explained what had just taken place; but to my surprise, all three were completely calm, relieved to be back on the ground, I'm sure.

It wasn't until years after that incident that Andrea disclosed to me that at the moment the engine lost power, she doesn't remember feeling scared. She trusted the problem would be solved, whatever it was. I find that interesting to hear, because even though I appeared to be calm and focused at the time, I wasn't sure of the outcome and was probably close to peeing in my pants.

It was clear to me that the lack of fuel pressure was the reason for the missing engine. Definitely it was not water in the fuel because in those cases, the failure is intermittent, not as it was then, subtle and progressive. And of course, it had nothing to do with the battery problem we had been experiencing since we left Panama. This was something else, and much more serious.

Chapter 29
Hindered

Once the Maule was secured, I began my search for *el Maestro*, a mechanic recommended by the tower controller. Once I found el Maestro, an elderly gentleman, he followed me slowly back to the airplane carrying a few basic tools in an empty plastic ice cream container. After hearing what had transpired, he removed the engine cowling and as soon as he saw the engine, he said: "Oooh, *mi Comandante*. This is a very complicated engine. I only work on engines with carburetors. You'll have to find someone else that knows about injector engines. *El Güero* is the one who works on these modern engines around here. I'll get him for you."

After a while, el Güero Aguirre arrived with his assistant *el Zorro* in a Chevrolet pickup camper. Again, I ran through what had happened and as soon as I finished, Güero spurted: "It's the mechanical fuel pump that failed. Not to worry, right away we'll take it down and repair it. Zorro, take out the blanket and lay it on the *troka* bed."

As Zorro prepared to spread the wool blanket on the camper bed, I asked Güero, "Why the blanket?"

"It's so that when we open the fuel pump, which has lots of springs, we don't lose any when they fly out."

Okay, that sounded reasonable to me.

I sent Pat and the kids by taxi to a hotel in downtown Los Mochis, but I stayed with the mechanics to see first hand what they were going to do to with the pump.

As I watched them ceremonially remove the mechanical fuel pump, I leaned against the Maule to reassess what had just happened: Engine failure on takeoff. Holy shit. I'm just glad I had read and understood the engine's operating manual. If not, another outcome would have probably taken place here today. And of course, it must be that I'm in good graces with the Big Guy up there for this to have happened without major consequences. But reflections were for another moment. Right now, I had to mentally relax and be prepared to make important decisions.

By eight o'clock the sky began to darken, and Güero tells me that they will continue working at the hotel. They grabbed the wool beige blanket by each of the four corners and picked it up with all the screws, nuts, washers, springs, gaskets and whatever else and tied the ends. I rode with them to their hotel that was in the center of town near the one where Pat and the kids were staying.

"The pump's got an air leak and that's why it can't maintain constant fuel pressure," Güero briefed me on the way to the hotel. Not having much experience with injection engines, like el Maestro, I didn't comment, just nodded. On that 30-kilometer ride to town I found out they were from Culiacan and were here on contract hired by a Los Mochis spraying outfit. I also learned, much to my surprise, that in the State of Sinaloa alone there were approximately 200 crop dusting airplanes. I mentally began to calculate how many crop dusters there were throughout all of Panama, and I couldn't get past twenty-five, including helicopters. Damn! Mexico is huge in comparison to Panama.

It was after eleven that night when I left them in their hotel room. They were sanding the base of the pump on a large mirror that had been taken from the wall to use as a flat surface. They assured me that the pump would be repaired that same night, and we agreed that they would let me know the next day when the pump was installed and to test it on the engine.

In Mexico, at least in Los Mochis, the day starts around midmorning, but by the same token, it ends late at night. Everything is open: stores, workshops, restaurants and even mechanics repairing fuel pumps using hotel beds as work benches.

In the morning, when I finally managed to find somewhere I could get a cup of coffee, it was well after eight. To kill time until I got a phone call from them that the fuel pump was installed, I sat down and reread the manufacturer's operations manual for the engine. I had done the right thing in that emergency. I felt better. About ten o'clock the streets suddenly began to fill with cars and hoards of people shopping and hurrying to work, making it difficult to walk on the sidewalks.

Shortly before noon, I get the anxiously awaited call at the hotel that the pump is ready for testing. I take a taxi to the airport by myself, with the conviction that if everything goes well, I'll return to pick up the family to continue on to Hermosillo. When I try the engine, it starts, but when I accelerate it, I realize it's not giving the power it should. The RPMs are constant but not as many as I should have in a static run-up. Shit!

"We have to send it to my *compadre's* shop in Chihuahua. His specialty is repairing these mechanical fuel pumps," Güero insists with faith.

"Chihuahua, how far is that?"

"Well, just on the other side of the *Sierra*. Just about a two-hour flight, no more."

"What flight, if my plane's grounded?" I ask, obviously frustrated.

"Ah, well, you can get there in *El Chepe*; it leaves every morning and I guarantee you'll enjoy it. That trip is worth taking."

"What *Chepe*?" I ask.

"Well, the train. Go ahead and take a break and do some touring in Chihuahua, land of my ancestors."

Given we had no guarantee that the problem would be solved, Pat and I decided to send the kids via El Paso, Texas, to their grandparents on an Aero Mexico flight that same afternoon.

The next day we arrived at the train station at six in the morning for a seven o'clock departure. The hours passed and no train was in sight. There were no benches at the station so I got up off the concrete floor and approached an office window to ask the woman sitting there reading a newspaper what was the reason for the delay.

"It must be arriving soon. Just wait," she says.

Another hour passes and I get up again and say to her: "Look, *señora*, we have been waiting for four hours and there is no sign of any train. What's happening?"

"Ah, well look, it's that there's been a slight hold up. A bridge that's being repaired, and the train will be delayed a few hours. Better come tomorrow at the same time of departure."

What the hell! All this time she knew and didn't say a word to the passengers. So I became the rail company's spokesperson and informed the dozens of French, Japanese, Swiss, German and who knows how many tourists from other countries as well as the dozens of locals who were waiting patiently for the train, everyone sitting on a hard-surfaced concrete floor, that there would be a 24-hour delay. *Carajo!*

Chapter 30
Back on Track

Just as the spectacle of the Acapulco daring divers was an unplanned event, we had no idea of what was in store for us at this stage of the trip: An impressive railway ride on the Chihuahua Railroad of the Pacific (AKA *El Chepe*) crossing the Barranca del Cobre located between Los Mochis and Chihuahua through a series of ravines and tunnels in the Occidental Sierra Madre mountain range in northwestern Mexico. In its entirety, the canyon system is larger and deeper than the Grand Canyon of Arizona. The construction of this railroad began at the end of the 19th century, but it wasn't until 1961 that it was completed due to the difficulty of the land, sporadic revolutions and lack of financing. The 252-mile railroad consists of 39 bridges and 86 tunnels and the route takes approximately 15 hours from sea level in Los Mochis to an altitude of almost 5,000 feet in Chihuahua. It's considered one of the most spectacular rail crossings in the world, which includes the Trans-Siberian railway in Russia, the Marrakech Express in Morocco, and the Cuzco to Machu Picchu train in Peru.

While that trip was spectacular, it was also rather daunting. Once the train left the Los Mochis station, it started to climb to cross the Sierra Madre. After a couple of hours, the train slowed to a snail's pace so I stuck my head out the open window to see why. I could see we were about to cross a long bridge, about a half-mile long, over a deep gorge of at least 1,000 feet. It brought to mind the Road Runner and the Coyote TV cartoons from years ago.

I turned to the purser, whom we had nicknamed Anthony Quinn because of his resemblance to the famous actor and asked, "Hey, Antonio, why are we going so slow?"

"Ah, this bridge. It's the one that was repaired yesterday."

"But why so slow, is it that they're not sure that it was well repaired?"

"*Pos sí*, of course it was well repaired. But you know, just in case..."

Miércoles! I thought to myself and put my head back inside the car. I didn't share that revelation with Pat until years later.

The train stopped in Creel, a picturesque village in the Tarahumara Mountains at an elevation of 8,060 feet, and the highest point of the crossing, where we spent the night and did some sightseeing. We continued the next day on to Chihuahua, this time a little faster since we were traveling downhill.

Chihuahua is a city with over a million inhabitants and a rich historical past from Mexico's War of Independence campaigns; the occupation by US military forces during the Mexican-American War; the capital of the exiled Benito Juarez government during the French Invasion; and the base of operations of the División del Norte, commanded by Pancho Villa during the Mexican Revolution.

Once in Chihuahua, we went to the shop to see where the fuel pump was being overhauled. Güero and Zorro had hopped a flight and were already there. I was satisfied and impressed with the shop layout and work ethics that I observed. At Güero's recommendation, we took advantage of our stay in the city and visited the Museo de la Revolución, and just as he had assured us, his paternal great-grandfather, General Aguirre, who had been Pancho Villa's lieutenant, appeared in a famous photograph of General Villa's General Staff. It was easy to find his ancestor in the collection of photos in the museum. The resemblance to el Güero was notable mainly because of the fair complexion among men with faces darkened by the sun. In Mexico, a fair-skinned person is referred to as *Güero*.

Even though the pump worked as expected on the test work bench, there was no guarantee that that would solve the problem on the airplane, so I decided that Pat should travel to Louisiana on a commercial flight, and I would go back to Los Mochis in *El Chepe*, and if the repairs to the pump worked out, I would fly the Maule without the touristic layovers we had originally planned. If it didn't work, then I would have to determine what to do next.

The trip back was quite boring, since the charm of seeing the Copper Canyon for the first time had been lost, and I was extremely anxious to continue the trip in the Maule. Los Mochis, even though a thriving, bustling city, had also outlived its charm.

The train arrived at the Los Mochis station at night, and the next morning I went directly to Güero and Zorro's hotel to get them on their way to the airport and have them install the repaired pump. Of course they were still in bed, and once we got on the road in their pick up, Güero informs me that they first needed to go to another *compadre's* house where their tools were kept. When we arrived at the *compadre's* house, the wife was just serving a hearty breakfast of *huevos rancheros*, *tortillas*, beans, and everything else that went with that spread. We were invited to join them. I had had coffee so I thanked them and just sat down at the table and accompanied them. At the end of the breakfast, Güero turns to Zorro and says:

"*Zorrito*, get in the *troka* and get us some *faros* because I ran out."

"Wait, Güero, what's this about *faros*? What are *faros*? Where's Zorro going? Weren't we leaving for the airport?"

"No, no, *mi Comandante*, it's that I ran out of cigarettes and after a breakfast like this one, it merits to finish it off with a little smoke. He'll be right back. *Tranquilo*."

I had trouble hiding my impatience, but I managed, listening to talk about issues that focused on airplanes. Finally, after all four of them finished smoking, we three headed to the airport. I left them installing the pump on the engine and went to pay the parking and landing fees and to present my flight plan, VFR direct to Hermosillo! I was confident that everything would go according to plan. When I returned to the tarmac, the engine was ready for the test run and Güero tells me: "*Adelante pues, mi Comandante, ándele*."

I turn the key to activate the starter and the propeller turns vigorously, but the engine doesn't start. *Nada!* I try again and nothing. *Mierda, coño!* Now what? Before it was that the engine wouldn't give the required RPMs, but now, it won't even start. After several attempts and nothing, I notice the look of despair on Güero's face and he says: "Let's go to the terminal to phone my *compadre* in Chihuahua. He must know what's happening. We tested it on the bench and it checked out. You were there too"

Once he got a line connection, I could hear Güero speaking on the phone: "*Compadre?* I installed the *chingada* pump but it doesn't suck fuel. ... How do you mean, *compadre*? Charlie Charlie Whiskey (CCW)? Not Charlie Whiskey (CW)? I don't know, *compadre*, I think so, but let me go and check and if it isn't, I'll invert it. Charlie Charlie Whiskey, right?"

All this time I'm understanding that it could be that the

pump was set backwards, that is, to rotate clockwise (CW) and that it should have been set to rotate counterclockwise (CCW). We head back to the plane over the extremely hot tarmac and they pull the fuel pump out, and with a screwdriver turn a screw head 180°.

"*Listo, mi Comandante*, this time if it doesn't work, I quit fixing airplanes."

"Are you sure about that, Güero?" I ask skeptically as I settle into my seat.

"*Pos sí*, It'll work. I don't doubt it for a second. You'll see."

I prime the injectors with the electric pump and turn the start switch, and the engine starts at once. I let it warm up at low RPMs and as soon as the oil temperature gauge is in the yellow, I slowly advance it to maximum takeoff power, and it works like it should. Holy shit! The problem's fixed!

I shut down feeling elated. I pay him with the last of my Mexican currency, and I offer him my multi-use Swiss knife, which he had been admiring, in appreciation for such diligent work. We close the deal and shake hands.

"But wait, *mi Comandante*, I have to accompany you on the test flight and sign the log certifying that everything is satisfactory so that you can then leave."

"What? Look, Güero, if you get on this airplane with me, you don't get off until we get to Hermosillo. Listen well, if I take off, I won't return. You decide, but I'm leaving right now, with or without you."

El Güero acceded and the last I saw of him he was waving from the ground as I spun the Maule around to take off. That little black airplane lunged into the air, and we were back on track.

Chapter 31
Energized Plane and Pilot

Los Mochis remained behind as I climbed heading north about five in the afternoon that Saturday. During the more than three-hour flight the engine behaved like a charm, as well as could be expected. I felt confident and relieved that the problem had been solved. As I flew over arid terrain, flat and devoid of trees, away from the coastline to my left, I reassessed: I've had enough nerve-wracking surprises to last me for a long, long time. From now on, I deserve a trip without traumas of any kind. I'm just going to sit back and enjoy the solace from up here, feeling the smooth running engine through the rudder pedals, the yoke and, most importantly, the seat of my pants.

I landed in Hermosillo as the sun had already set and it was beginning to get dark. There were no shops open to leave the battery charging, as had become my rule after landing on the last leg of the day's flight. I had deduced that after three hours of flight, I'd have trouble with the starter. I checked in a nearby hotel and that night before turning in, I began to study the route for the following day. Since this route wasn't the one originally chosen, I wasn't familiar with its characteristics. From my chart I could see that I would be flying between the two mountain ranges of the Sierra Madre Occidental, in a valley whose floor rises as one follows it north. The peaks on both sides oscillate between 7,000 and 11,000 feet, but since I'd be flying in the center, parallel to both of them, I didn't anticipate problems. An altitude of 11,500 feet would be more than enough. My plan was to head straight north from Hermosillo flying over inhospitable terrain before entering the US through Arizona, where I would continue on towards Tucson; after which I would head east for several hours over southern Arizona, New Mexico and Texas deserts before getting to the Louisiana bayous. My final destination would be Abbeville, in southwest Louisiana. The flight time would depend on the endurance of my body and what weather I would encounter en route. I planned to gas up the Maule to its 75-gallon capacity to avoid unnecessary fueling stops. I would have seven and a half hours range. Could my bladder endure that long?

Early the next day, Sunday, when I looked out of the hotel window, what I saw was a cloudy gray sky with light rain. Hmm, I don't like this at all.

When I arrived at the airport terminal, I met up with a group of US pilots members of the Flying Doctors organization, whom I came to learn make periodic trips to Mexico and Central America on health assistance missions to indigenous groups in remote areas. Their conversation centered on a line of thunderstorms between Hermosillo and Tucson, also their destination. They had telephone contact with the Tucson Control Center and the forecasts were not good at the moment. They suggested I join them for breakfast in town to wait for the weather to improve. I had already had my usual traveling breakfast, coffee, but I did need to get to an ATM machine for cash, so I piled in one of the four taxis that were contracted for the short trip into town.

As we sat around the breakfast table, I picked up that their aircraft ranged from high performance single engine to multi-engine turboprops and everything in between. And all of them had state-of-the art navigation and communication equipment on board. They planned their return flight in an organized manner, placing the fastest planes to depart first. It was no surprise that the Maule placed last in the formation of eleven aircraft. Well, okay with me, letting them go ahead would pave my way through. I didn't have weather radar in the Maule, so I only had my two eyes to detect menacing weather.

At about eleven they called Tucson and got the latest area forecast and it was good to go. The storm should have dissipated by the time we would arrive at our destination. We piled again in several taxis back to the airport. There was still a light drizzle but the visibility had improved considerably. Since I was programmed to be taking off last, I had ample time to fuel up the Maule and do a thorough walk around. I was concerned that the night before I hadn't been able to leave the battery charging. Since that flight had exceeded the three hours limit that I had determined was the maximum before the battery lost charge, I decided to try starting it. The propeller turned but not fast enough to start the engine. *Mierda, carajo!* The drama continues… Yesterday's three-and-a-half hour flight had drained the battery. There was enough charge for the radios to work, but not enough charge to start the engine.

Being Sunday, all the shops were closed, but I managed to find an airport security guard, Chema, who offered to get me someone who could help me, but he wasn't off until midday so I'd have to wait another half hour. I was impatient so I decided to go do the paperwork at the terminal and get my passport stamped by the immigration officials, a requirement when exiting the country. With my passport stamped and ready to go, as I was walking to the tower to file my VFR flight plan for Tucson, I saw the first of the eleven planes taking off. It was a sleek twin-engine turbo prop, a Beechcraft B-90.

I finished the paperwork at exactly twelve o'clock. Chema and I boarded a taxi and we set off with him giving directions through a maze of wall-to-wall small houses in a neighborhood close to the airport. When we got to the house he was searching for, Chema got out and went to the front door and started calling: "*Micho, Micho!*"

A woman in her nightgown half opens the screen door and angrily shouts back: "Micho? What Micho?" Go look for him at the other one's house, and when you find him, tell the scum not to come back here again. Not even to think about it!"

A browbeaten Chema walked back to the taxi after his unexpected encounter with this angry, hostile woman. He claimed to know where the other lady friend lived, so we headed out. We drove to a house a few blocks away, but this time he didn't get out of the taxi but asked the driver to blow his horn instead. After what seemed an eternity, a woman, who looked like she had a bad hangover, came out. Chema politely said, "Good morning, *mi señora*, we're looking for Micho. They urgently need him at the airport. Please let him know we're here."

After a while, a shirtless Micho, who also looked like he'd just gone to bed after a nightlong binge, appeared in the doorway. He listened with half opened eyes as Chema narrated my dilemma. Then he said lamely that he'd be over once he had his breakfast.

"What?" I interject. "No, no way, *amigo*. I need you to come with me at once. I'll buy you breakfast after the work is done. *Venga.*"

Micho reluctantly agreed and went back inside the

house to finish dressing. After the breakfast experience in Los Mochis with Güero and Zorro, I wouldn't get myself in another situation like that again. As I sat in that taxi waiting, I thought that after a *Cuervo* (Crow) in Panama, a *Gavilán*, (Hawk) in David, and a *Zorro* (Fox) in Los Mochis, a *Micho* (Male cat) here in Hermosillo shouldn't come as a surprise to me. I silently snickered keeping that thought to myself of this colorful array of nicknames.

Micho joined us in the taxi, and on the way I describe the history of the starter motor and all that had been done. He doesn't say or ask anything. He just sits there looking straight ahead. I can't tell if it's his personality or the hangover, but from the smell of alcohol on his breath it was probably the second possibility. When we arrive at the airport, he heads directly to a hangar and comes back with a screwdriver and a pair of wire pliers and removes the Maule's engine cowling to get to the voltage regulator, which he detaches from the firewall, all this time without saying a word. He disconnects the battery and takes it to the hanger to have it charged. After a short while, he returns with another voltage regulator, which I insist on checking to make sure it's for a 12-volt battery, same as the Maule's. It is, but I notice that it's not new. It's used. I suspect that since it is Sunday and there's nowhere to purchase airplane parts, he either took it from another plane or from a stashing corner of used parts that every workshop seems to have.

The last of the Flying Doctors' planes has just left, and we still need to wait at least another hour for the battery to fully recharge. During the wait, we chat, and I learn from Chema that Micho has been working at the airport since he was a boy, but that he isn't a licensed mechanic, and in confidence whispers: "Look, *Comandante*, he works on all kinds of airplanes, even though he can't sign his own work, but he's good at what he does. I guarantee he'll solve your problem. You'll see."

That doesn't surprise me. I know a couple of mechanics that are respected in their field and aren't licensed either, such as Catito Jaen and David Blake back in Paitilla. Besides, at this stage of the game, what can I do but resign myself to his ability. Micho returns with the recharged battery. I install and connect it to the electrical system and give the starter a try. The prop turns vigorously and the engine starts at once. After the standard checks, I turn the engine off and pay Chema and Micho for their services.

"I'm afraid you'll have to have breakfast without me, because I need to get out of here as soon as possible. My delay is already going on 15 days," I tell them as I hand them some extra pesos for their promised breakfast. We shake hands, bid farewell, and I hop in the Maule eager to continue my journey.

While I'm climbing to 11,500 feet, I listen to the chatter among some of the Flying Doctors' planes that had taken off ahead of me. What I hear doesn't reassure me at all; some are asking for vectors to avoid bad weather; others requesting higher altitudes to fly over the cloud formations; others requesting IFR authorization and two have rerouted to other airports. As scheduled, I'm just entering what appears to be the wide valley in the middle of the Sierra Madre Occidental, and what I see ahead is only a dark wall. Below I can spot a northbound railroad track, which from the map that rests in my lap I know leads directly to the US-Mexico border. But I don't have a weather radar to evaluate the intensity of the bad weather ahead, nor do I have approach plates for the Tucson airport, or any airport for that matter, nor oxygen to fly at 15,000 feet, which I hear from the other pilots is the minimum en route altitude (MEA) for IFR flights, and lastly but just as important, this Maule is not equipped for instrument flights. So I have no choice but to return. *Mierda!*

At 7,000 feet I stop climbing and initiate a left 180° turn back to Hermosillo. While I reduce power to descend, I over shoot my reverse course on purpose to take a peek at what the weather is like behind and below by lifting my left wing. What I see leaves me dumbstruck. The visibility below the base of the clouds seems to be unlimited. I continue turning back towards the north descending to 5,000 feet. Down here at this altitude the path is completely clear, I can see for what seems 100 miles. No way I'm returning to Hermosillo! I'll continue with the original plan, only this time under the cloud base. I just have to follow the railway tracks. At this altitude no radio navigational aids are within reception. This type of navigation is known as piloting, i.e. flying by visual contact with the ground. It has certain advantages, as well as risks, and the pilot better know how to manage them.

I feel more confident now that the decision has been made based on the unlimited visibility and the orientation that the railroad track provides. I relax. Once in the valley, as I fly along, I notice that it's growing narrower. Flying in a valley in mountainous area there's always a possibility of being forced to turn around, and a 180° turn must be able to be done without risk of hitting the other side of the mountain range. But I know for a fact that if I have to reverse my course in this valley, the Maule can do it with no problem. When I test flew it prior to this trip, one of the trials was to determine its turning radius with full flaps, and its performance was impressive. It can turn on a dime. If an unforeseen circumstance requires a 180° turn, it's doable. But I have other factors to concentrate on at this moment.

I continue flying along the railroad, but soon I notice that although it's barely mid-afternoon, it's getting dark. I know it's because the mountain range to my left is blocking the afternoon sun and also that there's a solid cloud cover over us, making solar illumination scarce in this valley. I also notice that although the altimeter reads 4,000 feet above sea level, I am only about 500 above the ground. The terrain elevation has been steadily increasing, approaching the base of the clouds at 5,000 feet. I lower two notches of flaps just in case I have to make a sudden 180° reverse turn. I decide I'd better play it even safer and drop another notch of flaps to further reduce the speed, just in case. I have a world aeronautical chart (WAC) spread on the copilot's seat dating back to the 1960s. All of a sudden the likelihood that there've been structural changes in the terrain below that don't appear on this chart, such as bridges, antenna towers or power lines crossing the valley in my path, alarms me. Shit! Better not think about that and pay attention to what's ahead. I select the fourth and last notch of flaps to reduce the speed almost at a snail's pace. I concentrate on seeing downwards and forward.

I sneak a brief look at the map and see that the border is about ten miles away and there're two airports near each other; one on the Mexican side, and one on the US side: Both in towns named Nogales. I immediately decide to land at the nearest one, Nogales, Mexico, and wait out the weather. Better to be on the ground wishing to be flying than flying wishing to be on the ground. Wise saying. The chart has an airport tower frequency and my only hope is that after almost thirty years they've not changed it. I call the control tower and they answer at once. I inform them where I am and ask for landing instructions and vectors to the airport, hoping they might have me on radar. My intention is to land immediately, if possible.

"Do you have the railroad in sight?" the controller asks me.

"Yes, it's about 100 feet below," I respond.

"Good, follow it up to where the railroad makes a sharp turn to the right. At that point, keep going straight ahead and there you see Runway 34, which is at an elevation of 4,000 feet. Report runway in sight."

I say out loud to myself: 4,000, if I'm flying at 3,700!

A few minutes later, I see where the railway makes a 90° turn to the right so following the controller's instructions, I power up the engine to climb to what appears to be a plateau above my present altitude. When I climb the 300 feet to reach 4,000, I see the runway straight ahead just below the cloud base, and I only have to turn the airplane slightly to the left to a heading of 340° to line up, reduce power and land. Without descending a single foot, I'm on the ground. I taxi the Maule following the tower's instructions, park in front of the terminal and turn off the engine. I sit for a while assimilating everything that has just happened. And all this time I thought I had depleted my reserve of jolts.

An authoritative looking individual approaches and introduces himself as the Airport Commander. In Mexico, all controlled airports have a commander who serves as administrator and is usually a pilot.

"I'm the Airport Commander. Stop by my office to explain your unexpected appearance to this airport."

"Well, for me it's also been an unexpected stop since

my original destination was Tucson, Arizona, and now because of the weather I find myself here."

"Look, I understand your urgency to land here, but you're going to have to deal with immigration, and they don't understand about these things. I recommend that you get ready, as they'll want to fleece you."

With that introductory welcome, I was already dreading what I knew awaited me: Intransigent officials with authority and power but no intent of applying practicality or common sense to a problem.

I thank him for the warning and follow him as he leads me inside the airport terminal and indicates the immigration offices to me. The immigration official, an extremely heavy man with a Pancho Villa type mustache and dressed in a tight khaki uniform, is sitting behind a wooden desk carved with the emblem of the Mexican shield: A large eagle with its wings spread open.

"Give me your passport and sit down," he tells me bluntly, extending his hand to receive the documents. "What's a Panamanian citizen doing in Mexico flying an airplane without an entry permit?"

"Look, Officer, the thing is that I left this morning from..." I start to say.

"You left but now you're entering Mexico, and if you already left, you cannot use the same entry permit again, because you have already left."

"Ah, yes, something like that, but see, it's that..."

"But nothing. The plane stays here until you get an entry visa to enter Mexican territory. When you have that, then you can leave the country."

"And where am I going to get an entry permit here in Nogales on a Sunday?"

"Well no, you'll have to go to Ciudad Juarez and from

there cross to El Paso where there's a Mexican consulate and you can get the paperwork there."

"Ciudad Juarez? That's more than five hundred miles from here. Also as a Panamanian I don't need a visa to enter Mexico."

"You're right there, but your airplane does need permission to enter, so the airplane doesn't move from here; however, all can be arranged with a convincing *feria*."

"*Feria*, what's that?" I ask pretending not to understand what he's referring to.

He rubs his first finger and thumb together, smiles and says, "Bills, dollars, money."

"See here, Officer, I don't have a single peso on me. Let me go to the ATM that's outside and take some money out," I said, and without a single second delay, which to this day I still don't know what prompted me to do it, I stood up, leaned over and snatched my passport he had in his hands and hurried out of the office.

Just outside of the door the Airport Commander who must have been outside listening, says: "Go, go! Get the hell out of here if you don't want to get screwed. *Váyase!*"

As I rush out the front door of the terminal with my passport in hand, I hear the immigration officer's heavy desk slide across the floor, and I hear a shout: "*Deténgase!*"

Stop? No way in hell! I get to the ramp where the Maule is parked, jump in and give the starter key a twist. Ruuuumm! The engine starts right away.

As I swiftly taxi to get to the runway intersection, I see a khaki-dressed figure gesticulating with his hands and shouting something I couldn't hear. I don't care what he's saying. I don't wait to get to the beginning of the runway and apply full power right there a few hundred feet down the runway. I apply full flaps and the Maule just jumps up in the air and climbs like I'd never seen before. This little plane has just saved me from a modern day *bandido*.

Chapter 32
Duty Fulfilled

Once in the air, I heard the tower calling, asking for an explanation, which I gave him and then requested him to relay me a flight plan for Nogales, Arizona. His reply was that since I hadn't submitted a written flight plan with them, he couldn't do anything for me, to contact Tucson Control and gave me the frequency: "*Buen viaje y buena suerte, mi Comandante.*" In Mexico, all pilots are addressed as *comandante*.

I contact Tucson Control and they inform me that my window of entry to the US airspace has expired and they advise to again submit a request to enter the Designated Military Information Zone (DMIZ). They give me another frequency for entry approval where I then am informed that the waiting approval time will be two hours. That's fine with me, because over the Nogales, Mexico, airport, I see the Nogales, Arizona, airport; and I still have four hours of fuel on board. After a two-hour wait for an approval flight, I will still have a minimum of two hours reserve to land. I'm thankful I filled the tanks to their maximum capacity in Hermosillo. And as Captain Celso Gallimore of Rapsa would say: "Aviation gasoline has no weight, *amigo*." But most of all I feel relieved that after more than three hours of flight time that it took from Hermosillo, the engine started at once. In short, the replacement of the faulty regulator did the job charging the battery. *Micho verraco, carajo!*

Flying in circles within the Mexican airspace I'm tired but relaxed, most of all feeling alleviated after such an intense experience. It brings to mind the similar case flying in the 180 in 1982 with the Mexican immigration officials in Matamoros, except that the officer on that occasion was cooperative in every way. It must have been that being accompanied by family, empathy prevailed on their part, not as now, where traveling alone doesn't rate any consideration at all. So it seems.

It's already past eight o'clock and the sun starts to set in the west. Seems like I'm always finding myself flying at this time of the day: At dusk. I can distinguish the lights of the two communities with similar names, but separated by history, culture and by an imaginary line that determines the political border between them. I detect sporadic lightning strikes to the north. It seems to be getting more frequent. It doesn't matter, in thirty minutes the two hours will be fulfilled, and I'll be able to enter the DMIZ and land. The WAC chart indicates that the airport doesn't have a tower and that the runway lights activate by clicking the microphone button five times. I'm starting to see the lightning getting closer to my destination and I start to worry. I'm not familiar with the storm behavior in these latitudes. In the tropics they're intense but usually of short duration, but up here in this region, I don't know. And I can't risk crossing the DMIZ before time. I know that they have me under radar contact and to do so would surely mean a custom and immigration authorities fine and who knows what other penalization.

At last, the two hours have elapsed. I contact Tucson Control for the authorization, which they give me immediately. I descend directly toward the runway without entering in a landing pattern because the storm is a short distance from the opposite runway threshold. I can't delay the landing. I click the transmitter button five times and the runway lights turn on, illuminating the sides of the runway. Let's do it!

Shortly after I land and park in front of a small structure that I assume is the terminal building and turn off the engine, the sky opens up in all its intensity and it takes me by surprise. After about twenty minutes, the rain starts to diminish and I see that there are lights inside the terminal and a person is watching from the window. When the rain becomes a drizzle, the person approaches the plane wearing a raincoat and a black baseball cap carrying a long flashlight. He stops next to the door that I've already opened, shines the flashlight in my face, then moves the beam to the plane's registration number and from there to the Panamanian flag on the tail.

"Hotel Papa?" he asks referring to the letters H and P on the side of the fuselage, which is the international designation on all Panamanian airplanes. "Is this airplane from Panama?"

Self-conscious of having landed unannounced in the middle of a rainstorm, at night, and with a black painted airplane to boot, I reply: "Yes, Panama."

His cap bears the US Department of Immigration and Customs Enforcement (ICE) logo. He looks at me closely and then asks me: "Do you know Pancho Suarez?"

I knew a Pancho Suarez who was a Tex-Mex mechanic who had been stationed at Albrook Air Base and had remained in Panama working with Copa and was well known in the Panamanian aeronautical network. So I answered assertively: "Yes, I know Pancho Suarez."

"How about Chino Chong?" he asks as if he's conducting a polygraph test.

Shit! That name doesn't ring a bell, but I'm going to have to bluff my way here on this one.

"Yes," I answer, "I know Chino Chong."

"Well, hell, son! Come on in out of the rain," he eloquently suggests. While I follow him to the terminal, somewhat reassured because it seems he has good feelings toward both individuals, Pancho and Chino, whoever Chino may be.

Once inside the building, he tells me he had been stationed at Albrook Air Force Base with Pancho Suarez and met Chino Chong while training at the USAF's School of the Americas and that Chino was his best man when he married his wife from La Chorrera!

Holy shit! I sure as hell hope all is well between him and his wife. I don't need any more negative surprises falling on me after today's events. He gets on a computer and looks for the Maule registration but HP 705 doesn't appear as authorized to enter the US.

Mierda, that's all I need now! I know the fines for this infraction are in the thousands of dollars, so I ask him to call Tucson Center, which responds that yes, HP 705 had requested and was authorized to enter US airspace ten minutes ago. Whew! With that resolved, everything takes its normal course. Tucson Center, however, asks me to submit a report at the FAA offices the next day to explain the reason for my erratic entry into the US. Sure, okay, not a problem.

Pancho's and Chino's friend helps me secure the Maule and offers to take me to a motel to spend the night, and invites me the next day to his house to meet his wife, an invitation that I have to decline. I'm determined to leave early for Tucson and resume my already extended trip, which is still a seven-hour flight to my destination. I fly to Tucson and clear up any misconceptions that had arisen from my unorthodox entry to the US.

From Tucson to Louisiana the trip was interrupted in Amarillo, Texas, where I had to spend the night because of bad weather en route. It was the first night in many that I managed to really rest. I must say with great satisfaction that for the rest of the trip, the Maule's fuel pump and starter gave no more trouble. I hold in sincere respect the skills of my Mexican technicians: el Güero, el Zorro and el Micho.

After a few days, Al came to Abbeville and flew the Maule all over the south visiting friends and finally to Florida. That was the last I ever heard of it. We decided to sell it and somebody in New York State bought it. The adventures flying the Maule were wholesome, but a little too intense for me.

Above: The Maule M-5 after a successful test flight.

Below: The Maule M-5 attracts a crowd during a proving flight in Boca de Cupe, Darien, Panama.

Above: Celebration after the first flight. Front row: Kenny Wilson, Alfred Chase, Ibu and an aviation enthusiast. Back row: Tato Cuervo, Rodolfo Causadias, Edgardo Murillo and Betito Chavarria.

Below: Alfred Chase and Ibu with the restored Maule M-5.

Above: Ibu, Ramon Gavilan and Pillo Alvarado during a technical stopover. Enrique Malek Airport, David, Chiriqui, Panama.

Right above: Preparing the Maule M-5 for a flight to Tapachula, Mexico. Pavas airport, San Jose, Costa Rica.

Right center: Teo after a grueling six-hour flight from Pavas to Tapachula with a stopover in San Salvador, El Salvador.

Right below: Andrea ready to board the Maule M-5 in Puerto Escondido en route to Puerto Vallarta, Mexico.

The Maule 205

Above: Photograph in the Pancho Villa Museum in Chihuahua, Mexico. Pancho Villa is in the center, and el Güero Aguirre's great grandfather is on Pancho Villa's right.

Part 7
Aero Perlas

33 One More Rung
34 Captain's Stripes
35 Stressful Routine

Chapter 33
One More Rung

In the mid-1990s, Copa Airlines was experiencing a somewhat rapid growth and had begun to recruit pilots to crew their increasing fleet of Boeing 737s. In order to meet that need, it had relaxed the requirements for minimum flight hours, but even so, it required pilots to have time in turbine airplanes vs. piston engine airplanes. Aero Perlas was its biggest recruiting source, since it operated turbo-prop aircraft.

Aero Perlas, aware of the imminent loss of their pilots migrating to Copa to fly jets, put out flyers all over the airport offering a ground course for the De Havilland DHC-6, a Canadian twin-engine turbo-prop aircraft commonly known as a Twin Otter. The requirements for the course were a valid pilot's commercial license, with multi-engine and instrument ratings. I had just obtained my multi-engine certification so I met all three requirements. I talked Robert Katz, an aviator friend, into signing up for the course. He joined me in taking advantage of that rare opportunity. Classes were Monday to Friday from 6:00 to 10:00 in the evening for six weeks. Out of the approximately sixty candidates, most were recent graduates of aviation schools with few hours or veteran pilots like Victor Yard, with thousands of hours. In short, the competition would be stiff. Sergio Ortiz, a Shorts 3-60 captain flying for Aero Perlas was the instructor. The thoroughness and complexity of that course was such that after taking it, I never had any problems learning other large aircraft characteristics. Understanding the principles of hydraulic, electrical, mechanical and fuel systems, as well as the turbine engines and propellers, forced Robert and me to study in an organized manner since we both had full time jobs outside aviation. I don't remember having ever studied any subject in my entire scholastic career as hard as that initial course. In the end, Robert and I came out in the upper 5% of the class. Not bad, considering the competition.

It was a known fact that Aero Perlas would be selecting ten copilots to crew the Twin Otter, but it wasn't necessarily the top ten that were selected. When I didn't see my name among the chosen, I sought out George Porgy Novey, Aero Perlas's CEO and major shareholder, to state my case. I knew the airline was being forced to ask the DAC for extensions to pilot flying hours to be able to comply with their itineraries, especially with the flood of resigning pilots. I managed to convince Porgy of the advantage of having a qualified part-time pilot, me, to fill the gaps. He accepted on the condition that I would pay back the flight training with duty hours flown. Once checked out as copilot on the Twin Otter, I would fly 45 hours a month of the maximum 90 allowed by DAC. I started the twelve-hour flight training with Captain Raul Dominguez, who had been one of my instructors when I formally started my pilot career at La Escuelita in Paitilla. A week later I took my check ride with Carlos Lopez, also an Aero Perlas captain, and I was ready to start flying copilot in a twin-engine turbine airplane.

By then, I was older than most of the captains with whom I had to fly, but that didn't bother me. Even though I had more than 2,500 hours of which more than 95% were pilot-in-command (PIC), I didn't flaunt that fact. I wanted to assimilate as much knowledge as I could and learn the techniques, and Aero Perlas was an ideal school for it. Having so many solo-PIC hours made it difficult at first for me to adapt to being second in command, but after the required Crew Resource Management (CRM) training, I quickly fit in. The Twin Otter was an ideal airplane for the rugged region where it operated: San Blas and Darien. For me, that type of operation was enchanting, and when I was moved up to fly as a copilot of the Shorts, I left reluctantly. I was leaving behind the type of flight that was really made for me: Back country bush flying.

However, I knew that the customary rule was that Shorts copilots would eventually be upgraded to Twin Otter captains, so I accepted the change positively. In the Shorts, the routes flown were established and the flight operations were more closely regulated. The Shorts was a transport category aircraft, that is weighing more than 12,500 pounds and stricter adherence to the manufacturer's flight manual was required. It had a capacity for thirty-six passengers, and all flights were operated under IFR rules. The company had already started flights to San Jose, Costa Rica, three times a week, a refreshing change from the limited Panama, David, Bocas, Changuinola and Colon destinations. Eventually I was flying up to 60 hours per month and complying with my job with the Panama Canal. I flew after work on weekdays and all day on weekends and holidays and during my Panama Canal vacations. I often returned home at eight o'clock at night after a long day at my regular Canal job and from the last flights of the day. In those days the Trans isthmian highway, which connected Panama City with the Colon Free zone on the Caribbean coast, was in terrible condition so the Free Zone executives traveled by air. That created a high demand for flights late in the afternoon, and I was a regular crewmember on those flights.

But there were no complaints from me. I was doing what I liked and acquiring valuable experience on each flight. I soon realized that every flight was an education for me. I trained with captains willing to share their experiences and knowledge as were captains Milciades Jaen, Alfredo Williams, Victor Yard and Jaime Martinez. Each had his preferred method of operating, but I was able to acquire from all of them helpful guidelines that became part of my flight routine when eventually I was promoted to captain. Their personalities and styles varied, but what they did have in common was their attribute of sharing their expertise, and I profited greatly from it.

Chapter 34
Captain's Stripes

At an Aero Perlas Christmas party, Porgy Novey called me over and after some small talk, asked: "How do you feel flying the Shorts?"

"Comfortable," I said without hesitation.

Then and there he called Captain Ezequiel Suira, who was in charge of the company's training department, and told him that as of the first of January, I would begin training for the captaincy, not in the Twin Otter, but in the Shorts. Shit! That threw me off base. While I felt honored, I was somewhat disheartened. I had expected the captaincy to be in the Twin Otter, the bush-flying airplane. But hey, earning the four stripes of the captaincy is a goal of every copilot. How could I not accept? So my flight training for the Shorts captaincy began on January 1, 2000, in Gelabert Airport, recently relocated to Albrook under the guidance of Captain Suira, a professional and committed instructor pilot. I took my check ride fifteen days later with Captain Ismael Chacho de la Rosa, the Operations Chief. It was a hazy, bumpy, turbulent, crosswind-filled day. I passed. Talk about relieved and proud.

It's customary for a new captain to fly a hundred hours with an experienced captain as copilot, so the transition to command, Initial Operating Experience, (IOE), is smooth, but in my case, it was determined that the hours I had been flying as PIC in my 90 HP Cessna 140 exempted me from the 100-hour requirement with another captain in the right seat. I wasn't entirely convinced by that reasoning, but that's how it was. I flew my first flight as captain four days after I passed my check ride, and nowhere else but to Bocas, which of course included Changuinola, a somewhat precarious airport for the Shorts, which, though the name implies it, is not a STOL airplane at all. Operating the Shorts in Changuinola required special attention. The weight of the aircraft had to be restricted to ensure that the plane could stop within the available distance on a landing, and, in the case of a failed takeoff, stop within the remaining distance on the runway. The copilot assigned to me on that first flight was Johnny Wilson, who was considered a top-ranked copilot. Good choice. I felt comfortable on that first day in the left seat at the command of a transport category airplane. I had reached yet another rung in my aviation career.

I never went back to flying the Twin Otter, but I consider the three years I flew as captain in the Shorts, to have been where I learned the most about flying airplanes. Fifty percent of the flights were in Instrument Meteorological Conditions (IMC) since the Shorts, a non-pressurized aircraft with an operational ceiling[34-A] of only 10,000 feet didn't have the capacity to fly above bad weather. That factor forced us, in most cases, to have to fly in the "soup." The Shorts was equipped with weather radar and a basic GPS. All the ILS, VOR or ADF approaches were flown manually since there was no automatic pilot on board. This lack of up-to-date technology demanded that the pilots be competent in manual flying. In addition, it certainly helped to create confidence. Operating at El Coco Airport in San Jose, Costa Rica, at night, in rain or thick fog, and with the base of clouds at minimum legal heights was extremely stressful, and that's when I began to notice bits of gray in my hair. Those were the conditions encountered during the rainy season. More than once I remember circling in a holding pattern waiting for the Control Center's authorization for an approach, all the while listening to other airlines with all the latest technology on board assisting them and even so, having to miss the approach. I'd ask myself, what the hell am I doing here? And then suddenly I would hear: "Aero Perlas 421, authorized ILS 06 approach; report initial fix; visibility mile and a half, ceiling 200 feet; be advised Taca and Lacsa have both missed the approach with no runway contact."

Holy shit! What the hell am I doing here? I vigorously ask myself again. But, it's known that experience has its price, and in Aero Perlas, on those flights to San Jose during the rainy season, was where I acquired it. I became seasoned. Yes, it was expensive, but it was worth it if you take into account what I got: First-hand experience in hands-on flying and decision-making.

But all in all, I enjoyed that route and also experienced pleasant situations that come to mind, like when on a flight from San Jose to David my brother Neo and sister-in-law Chrys were on the flight unbeknownst to them that I was the captain. In mid-flight I left my seat and went to the passenger cabin to greet them. They were surprised for sure. When I invited my brother to the cockpit, some passenger started to get uneasy and demanded to know why a passenger was going into the cockpit, at which Chrys responded assertively: "Because the captain is my husband's brother." The regulation of restricting the cockpit to crewmembers only was not in effect yet.

When Taca acquired majority shares in Aero Perlas and started running the flight department, there were both operational changes and new routes added. The

Shorts flight crews were sent every six months to a simulator refresher course at La Guardia Airport in New York, and a stricter adherence to a newly implemented flight operations manual were applied. And Managua, Nicaragua, was a new destination. The flight began in David at five in the afternoon with El Coco as the first stopover to coincide with a Taca flight from Los Angeles, California. The Managua flight left San Jose at seven and returned at eleven o'clock that night, where the flight crew would overnight. When the Taca passengers first caught a glimpse of the Aero Perals Shorts waiting on the tarmac to transport them to Managua, there were typical comments such as: "What! We get off an Airbus jet to board a milk carton with propellers. Are you kidding me?" *No jodás!*

The airway between San Jose and Managua was Ambar 502, and the minimum en route altitude (MEA) was 11,000 feet. IFR flying regulations require an even thousand feet when flying between 181° and 360°, and require an odd thousand feet when flying between 1° and 180°. Since we were flying northwest, we had to fly at 12,000 feet. That was a difficult task for the Shorts. It eventually got there, but barely and under strain. The climb was slow, so by the time we reached that altitude, we were already fifty miles from Managua and Flight Control would authorize a lower altitude, which meant that only for brief moments we operated at more than 10,000 feet.

Not being pressurized, the airplane had oxygen masks, but only for the pilots. Once we passed 10,000 feet, we would don them for a short period since we soon began our descent to Sandino Airport in Managua. The flight attendants had to deal with the irritated passengers at the beginning of the flight, but when we reached cruise altitude, their irritation subsided considerably.

On one of those flights to Managua, with a planeload of US missionaries, we waited at the end of the runway for over an hour for takeoff clearance due to below minimum runway visibility. We finally were authorized to leave San Jose with the fog almost down to the floor. Fifty miles out of the Managua VOR, we could see the city lights in the distance and the Sandino Airport beacon. It was a dark night. About ten miles away, we began to see lightning strikes near the airport. As we flew over the VOR and started a procedure turn to capture the ILS glide slope, the lightning strikes became more frequent and seemed to be over the airport. Once established on the glide slope and with the before-landing checklist completed, we suddenly experienced a series of vertical up-and-down drafts commonly known as wind shear. It was so strong that the airplane's speed couldn't stay constant; it would climb and descend abruptly and rock from side to side with steep banks approaching 45°. Precisely at that time, we lost all visual contact with the runway lights because of the heavy downpour. While I tried to prevent the steep banks with my left hand on the control wheel, with my right hand I worked the power controls to counteract the violent ascents and descents, and with both feet on the rudder pedals trying to maintain course, we managed to keep from losing control of the airplane.

Within seconds of reaching the decision altitude (DA), which is the moment the pilot decides whether to continue with or miss the approach, the copilot called out runway lights in sight so we continued the landing approach. No sooner had the tires touched the runway, than we saw lightning strike the terminal building. Suddenly the runway lights, taxi lights, ramp lights and the terminal building lights went black, as did all lights in the surrounding area. Unable to see the runway or taxiway to proceed to the parking ramp, we had to stop in the middle of the runway to wait for the storm to pass, or for the lights to come back on. Soon an official car with flashing lights approached us intending to guide us to the ramp, but it was obvious that the driver had no idea where the taxiway was either, so I decided to stay where we were and turned the engines off. As I entered the passengers' cabin to inform them of what was going on, they spontaneously burst into applause and broke out in a hymn of praise for having gotten safely out of this predicament. Later, when the electric current was restored, we started the engines and taxied to the front of the terminal. When the flight attendant opened the door for the passengers, they stepped out into ankle-deep water. However, that didn't faze the grateful passengers at all. They were on the ground. Wet, but on the ground. My copilot on that flight, Gustavo Cunningham, was instrumental in helping maintain the plane under control at that critical moment mainly by his composure during that ordeal. Even today when we meet, we instinctively reference that Managua odyssey.

What made matters worse that night was that the flight didn't end there in Managua; the return trip to San Jose was programmed to leave at ten o'clock. On the way back, good weather conditions were reported for El Coco and when approaching from afar, you could see the Runway End Identification Lights (REIL). But at the last minute, the airport closed operations because a thick layer of ground fog from 0 to 1,000 feet had rolled in. Zero visibility and zero ceiling. The Control Center gave us the option of entering in a waiting holding pattern or going to our alternate airport, Liberia, near the Pacific coast. I opted for the second. I had learned that when the wind was calm, that fog would take hours to dissipate. When we arrived at Liberia, there was no place to park. Most flights bound for El Coco had opted for the same, wait it out on the ground by taking refuge in Liberia. We were sent to the end of the runway's taxiway, and it wasn't until two hours later that we got cleared to continue to San Jose. The approach and landing were uneventful in extreme visual conditions, and when we finally arrived at the hotel I asked myself, although in a much calmer circumstance: What the hell am I doing here? But then, I knew the answer to that question.

Chapter 35
Stressful Routine

Flying safely requires a clear and timely temperament and analysis. Situations sometimes arise where there are no ideal options. Even if the preflight preparation and the en route planning have been meticulous, you can find yourself in a situation where the options at hand have risks. That's when determining the best of these options and executing the plan comes into play, without any hesitation.

Several times after that Managua experience, I asked myself: Why didn't I abandon the approach when entering that intense storm? Had I done so, wouldn't it have been better? Maybe, but recreating the circumstances of that night I've come to the conclusion that it was because of the precarious control we had over the plane, and that if we had tried to suddenly change the plane's configuration, which was extended flaps, landing gear down at approach speed, and at a descent angle, it would have caused us major control problems. It was a momentary decision yes, but in aviation one must know in depth one's limitations as well as those of the aircraft while processing information from external influences as was the prevailing weather in this case. In a critical situation like that one that night, there's no time to analyze factors in a weighted manner before making a decision. The time available to make decisions is counted in seconds.

In 2000, when Panama took over the administration of the Panama Canal, the management employees who would continue with the Panamanian Canal had already been selected and invited to join the new administration. I was one of them, and to top it off, I was promoted to manage a new division, the Environmental Division. Here things got complicated for me because that meant that in addition to new and greater responsibilities, I would have a work schedule that now required not eight but up to twelve consecutive hours of performance. At the beginning I had to quit taking the afternoon flights to Colon during the week because of this new work culture. I flew only on weekends and holidays, depending on my Canal responsibilities. By agreeing to be part of the new Canal team, my commitment would be for a minimum of three years, I found myself at a crossroads for the third time. To fulfill my personal obligations along with those of the Canal and Aero Perlas required rigorous coordination and planning. Honestly, I don't know how I managed to organize myself to maintain such responsibilities, but I did. I flew for two more years, until the pitcher overflowed.

One Sunday, I had the following itinerary: In the morning, Panama – Bocas – Changuinola – Bocas – Panama, and again the same in the afternoon. I remember that when I landed in Changuinola for the second time that day, I remained seated in the Shorts's cockpit while the airplane was on the ground. Likki Man, an Atopan mechanic and a childhood acquaintance, approached the cockpit window: "*Ey Ibu, yu no gwain get down? Whappin?*"

That question sounded strange to me because I always disembarked to chat with the ground crew, especially in Changuinola, where I knew them from years back. But that afternoon I felt tired and drained of energy.

"No man. Not today. *I is taiard to ras, buay.*"

Once the flight plan and weight and balance calculations were reviewed, signed and returned to the Station

Manager, I began the takeoff briefing, as is customary in transport type airplanes before takeoff, and consists of reviewing out loud what actions each of the pilots should take if an emergency arises before, during or after the decision speed (V1). The pilot who is going to take off does this.

In mid-briefing the copilot interrupted me: "Captain, are you going to fly this leg?"

"Yes, why?"

"It's that you flew the leg from Panama to Bocas and then from Bocas to Changuinola."

"I landed here in Changuinola?"

"Yes. You flew the leg here to Changuinola also. Isn't it my turn to fly?"

In most airline operations, once the copilot has demonstrated ability in the cockpit, the legs are shared, but at the captain's discretion. The copilot that day was highly competent. We normally would have shared the legs.

I had no recollection of having landed. The Changuinola runway was not one to take lightly with the Shorts. One needed to exercise caution, precision and concentration. At once I nodded and told the copilot that yes, he would be the pilot flying. When we landed in Bocas after a short seven minutes flight, I also gave him the leg to Panama, and during the whole flight back I consciously analyzed what had happened. If I had landed and not even been aware of it, this meant that I had done it by rote, unknowingly. Crap! That was serious. Right then and there I knew what I had to do. I couldn't allow this to happen ever again, placing passengers, crew and the airplane at risk. Stop flying! That was my last flight in Aero Perlas. The next day, I handed in my resignation letter to management. It took my body and mind over two months to break the regime I had subjected them to over the past six years. As much as I was seduced by flying, that was a necessary and decisive decision. I was physically and mentally exhausted.

Aero Perlas 227

Above left: Ibu after his first flight as copilot in Aero Perlas's Twin Otter.

Below left: Ibu commanding the Shorts 3-60 en route to Managua, Nicaragua.

Below 1: The Shorts 3-60 taking off from David, Chiriqui, Panama.

Below 2: Ibu, Denise Vergara, Raul Arosemena and Anastas Arcia. Aero Perlas crews. Paitilla, Panama.

Above: Ibu with Captain Ismael Chacho de la Rosa after passing his check ride for captain in the Shorts 3-60. Albrook, Panama.

Right: Ibu training in the Shorts 3-60 simulator. LaGuardia Airport, New York, USA.

Above 1: Gabriel Him, Roberto Vallarino and Ibu. Twin Otter DHC-6 in Paitilla, Panama.
Above 2: Ibu, Orlando Miller, Bocas del Toro professional baseball player, Julissa Brocham and Anastas Arcia. Paitilla, Panama.
Below: Ibu on his first day as captain of the Shorts 3-60. Changuinola, Panama.

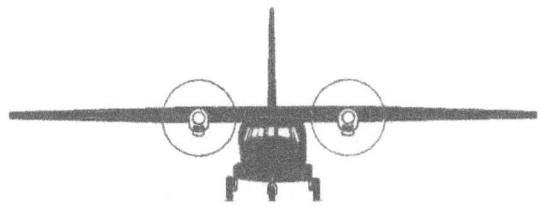

Part 8
Evergreen International Airlines

36 Recruitment and Training
37 Getting Acclimatized
38 Woes of the Captaincy
39 Mexican Stopover
40 Mission Rejected
41 End of a Dream

Chapter 36
Recruitment and Training

After I left Aero Perlas, it took me a long time and a lot of effort to reprogram my life. I became solely dedicated to my responsibilities with the Canal and in my spare time to flying my Cessna 140.

Unexpectedly one afternoon I received a call from the Air Panama Regional offices, a cargo and passenger company recently formed by the former shareholders of Aero Perlas. It was Captain Raul Dominguez, their Chief of Operations. He told me about their plans to acquire Fokker F-27 airplanes to fly both national and international routes and they were looking for captains to crew them. They were offering a course on the airplane systems and invited me to attend. It was definitely an offer that I gave lots of consideration. I had already fulfilled and exceeded my three-year commitment with ACP; the Environmental Division under my responsibility had completed the socio-environmental studies for the proposed expansion of the Canal; and I just wanted to venture full time into something that I was passionate about. Flying.

I decided to resign from the Canal and signed up for the F-27 course. Besides myself, all the other pilots taking the course flew Twin Otters and Islanders for Air Panama Regional. I ended up as one of the five chosen for captain training in the F-27. A few days before I was scheduled to initiate flight training conducted by an Argentine flight instructor, I found out by chance, that there was manifest discomfort among the company pilots who had not been chosen for captaincy training. They were disgruntled that "outsiders" were chosen over them to be trained for the left seat. I was the only "outsider" so I meditated on that situation carefully. I fully understood their feelings since they had been with the company from the start, and now felt ignored and passed over. I didn't see myself in a circle of resentment among colleagues, and I decided to decline the offer for that left seat. As much as I wanted to fly, it wasn't worth it. In addition, and equally as important, I'd be flying the same well-known routes, to the same destinations, and following the same routine. That was not what I wanted to do at this stage of my life.

As I found myself without any work commitment, and was trying to get used to start the day without the myriad responsibilities that ruled it until recently, I received a call from Anchorage, Alaska, around nine o'clock one night. The person on the other end of the line identified himself as the Chief Operating Officer of Evergreen Helicopters of Alaska (EHA), a subsidiary of Evergreen International Airlines (EIA). He was interested in interviewing me for a possible pilot job. An airline ticket from Panama to Anchorage was waiting for me at the Continental Airlines counter in Panama City.

I was unsure what this call was all about. Then it hit me. Weeks before, through Hugo Giraud of Mapiex, I had met Javier, who flew for EHA operations in Panama. When Hugo introduced us, he told Javier I had flown the Shorts in Aero Perlas. He, Javier, was going to take an EHA plane for a test flight and invited me along. The airplane was one of four that EHA operated from Panama and was a Spanish built twin-engine turbo-prop, a Casa 212-200. The test flight took about an hour, including takeoffs and landings from the left side that Javier generously ceded to me. After flying the Shorts and the Twin Otter, the Casa

212 was an easy airplane to fly. When we returned to the hangar, Javier told me that he'd have me in mind if a pilot vacancy came up. I thanked him for the opportunity to fly the Casa 212 and that was it. I never thought about it again. Until that night when I received the call from Anchorage.

I hung up the phone and began to reassess the conversation and realized that the flight with Javier weeks earlier had most likely been an evaluation. The night of the call we were in Boquete, and encouraged by Pat to go to the interview, we left the next day in the Cessna140 for Panama City, and the day after that I was on my way to Anchorage, Alaska. I arrived at about ten o'clock at night, Anchorage time, but it was as bright as if it were midday. Rays of sunlight slipped through the hotel curtains and when I got up the next morning, I felt as if I had not gone to bed at all. My inner clock was out of phase.

When I arrived at the office for the interview, there were several candidates in the waiting room, all experienced pilots, most retired military. I had the bad luck to be the first interviewed, so I had no idea what to expect. The interviewers were the Director of Operations with whom I had talked to over the phone and the Vice President of Operations. Both were line pilots. I was briefed that the operation consisted of an EHA contract with the United States Army Southern Command (SOUTHCOM), based in Panama; supervised by the Department of Defense (DoD); monitored by the USAF; and regulated by the FAA being that the aircraft were operating under civilian regulations.

EHA operated throughout Central America, the Caribbean and parts of South America; anywhere there was a SOUTHCOM presence. There were no longer flights to

Venezuela or Bolivia due to the estrangement between the governments of those two countries and the US. After recounting my pilot experience, I was taken aback when they asked me what salary I aspired. I was unprepared to answer that question. I stuttered a bit but immediately remembered Aero Perlas salaries where a copilot earned nine hundred dollars a month in the Twin Otter and a novice Shorts captain started at a thousand eight hundred dollars, so I answered, two thousand dollars. Gulp.

They looked at each other and one of them shook his head and said: "No way. We're going to pay you four thousand as base salary, plus fifteen hundred for living expenses, plus travel expenses when outside Panama, and fifteen percent hazardous pay, but under the condition that after three months you checkout as a captain. Then your base salary will be seven thousand dollars plus the rest, of course."

I was silent for a moment before agreeing by nodding my head and answering: "Yes, of course, I accept, I do."

What was there not to accept, but I did have doubts about that hazardous flights thing. Would that be the reason for such attractive remuneration?

"What does hazardous flights entail?" I asked.

"Ah, that. That's when transporting hazardous material or operating in areas known to have subversive activity. We're still working on getting that approved." I soon learned that most of the flights would be in Colombia in support of Plan Colombia.[36-A]

Of the seven candidates, four of us were chosen: Two for Panama, one for the Philippines and one for Sudan in Africa. As a pre-hiring condition, we were required first to pass an anti-doping test. Then, if we passed that, we had to comply with on board fire control and hazardous materials handling as well as to take an advanced aviation test on the Internet that took over 16 hours and were given three days to comply. As the operation would be governed under Part 135 of the FAA regulations, i.e. on-demand charter and cargo, non-itinerary flights, which didn't include flight attendants, we also received first aid and cardiopulmonary resuscitation training. Finally, we were sent to Lafayette, Louisiana, to conform to a required two-day dunking course, which included a mandatory successful exit from a submerged aircraft cabin at a depth of 30 feet in a pool. The ditching I had experienced in Nargana didn't prepare me at all for this, as I initially thought. That ditching had been a piece of cake comparatively, mainly because here you had to hold your breath for 30 to 45 seconds until the cabin settled in the bottom and rolled on its side before you could initiate the exit. Candidates who panic and can't hold their breath until then and have to be rescued by divers with air tanks fail. There's no doubt that this course was the most extreme of all I've had in aviation. Definitively, this was not something anyone who suffers from claustrophobia wants to be exposed to. How I missed the Aero Perlas crewmembers' requirement at the Adan Gordon pool: "Okay, everybody in the water and swim out to the raft and get in! Excellent. Now you can go get dressed." It took a lot of effort and moments of anxiety, but I qualified. Of the dozen or so candidates, not everyone was so lucky.

Because my Airline Transport Pilot's (ATP) license was Panamanian-issued and I'd be flying US registered airplanes, I had to stop off in Atlanta, Georgia, for a few days to get the FAA equivalent. While there, on the last day of that training, I had an experience that almost washed me out. I had already satisfactorily passed my written and oral examinations and was taking my flight check ride in a twin-engine airplane. I had demonstrated the in-flight emergency maneuvers, had satisfactorily executed the four IFR approaches, when finally the flight examiner informed me that we could return to base and asked me for a short field landing. Right away I knew the check ride had been successful. I don't know if the notion of success or what carried me away. I lined up with the runway, applied full flaps and slowed the plane down, hanging from the prop. I set the tires right at the beginning of the runway with the skill and grace of the best Paitilla bush pilot, and stopped the plane at an impressive short distance. Once I saw the examiner's face, I realized that I had screwed up. He never said a word. When we entered his office he handed me a pamphlet and told me that what I had done was not a short field landing, but a foolhardy act. He made me read in the ATP flight test guide out loud where a short field landing is described. I had touched down a good distance before the designated Runway Touchdown Zone Markings.[36-B] I failed the ride and I had to fly an additional two hours practicing short field landings with an instructor before sitting for another check ride. To this day, I don't know whether to blame my flying in San Blas and Darien, my landings in the Shorts in Changuinola, not having carefully read the FAA guide for ATP flight test requirements or what. The fact is that I had to stay an extra day to re-demonstrate my ability in "short field" landings, but this time adhering strictly to FAA guidelines.

Once I obtained my ATP license, I assumed that I had complied with everything required for the job. I didn't know that there was still something missing that would take more than three years of paperwork: the background check conducted by the DoD. The investigation consisted of filling out dozens of forms with information about my family, my friends, my travels, my political and personal preferences and lots more. The irony was that when I left EHA in 2009, I was still being asked for information related to my security clearance.

Chapter 37
Getting Acclimatized

My first tour as a line copilot was to Bogota, Colombia. Once in Bogota, the day began with a very early morning breakfast and transport in a bulletproof van to the Colombian Military Transport Air Command (CATAM) at El Dorado Airport where our plane was parked. When we got off in front of the military terminal and proceeded to submit our flight plan, I heard a uniformed soldier address me: "Commander, do you want me to tow your *Herculito*?"

Meecho! What's with this guy? His question took me by surprise and I didn't know what to make of it. In Spanish the word "Herculito" sounds very much like *el culito*, which literally means little butt. Was he joking or just being uncouth? Either way, it didn't sit well. I gave him a dirty look and just kept walking without answering. After takeoff when we settled to our cruise altitude, and I finished transmitting the HF radio reports to Mohan-Davis Air Force Base in Arizona which recounted our altitude, speed, heading, cargo on board, crew, estimated time en route (ETE), estimated time of arrival (ETA) and atmospheric conditions, I asked Moises, who was the captain on that flight: "*Oye*, Moises, what was that Herculito crap all about with that soldier back at the terminal?"

Moises laughed and explained that this was how the Colombian soldiers referred to our Casa 212 because of its resemblance to the Lockheed Hercules C-130 aircraft but with two engines instead of four. Oh, so that was it. Now I understood. The airplanes were slightly similar except in the size and number of engines. The Casa 212 was a link in the chain that began with the large USAF freighters, the Globemaster C-17s and the Galaxy C-5s, which flew in large metal cargo containers to CATAM, where they were distributed to the Colombian Air Force Hercules to transport to outlying runways. The Whales, the Hercules and the Herculitos (small Hercules), in that order. I made a mental note to apologize to the soldier for my curt response once we got back to CATAM. I had misunderstood him, but I never saw him again.

That night at the hotel I felt that although my first day had had a bad start because of the *Herculito* misunderstanding, it had ended well. I had flown to out-of-the-way settings such as the Colombian Military Training Center in Tolemaida, San Vicente del Caguan; at one time center of the demilitarized zone created by the Colombian government as a safe haven for FARC rebels from 1998 to 2002, and La Macarena; a town that in 2010 came under the international spotlight for allegations of extra judicial killings of FARC sympathizers by the Colombian military. Each one of those places bore an attention-grabbing history that I'd get to know even better over time.

On the third day of this six-day mission, when we returned to Bogota after a flight to Arauca near the Venezuelan border, there were instructions for me to wait for another Casa 212 arriving from Panama. I was to replace that copilot and proceed on to Guayaquil, Ecuador, to fly a mission the next day. We left Bogota late in the afternoon and arrived as the sun was setting in Guayaquil. Our assigned parking was in the military compound across the Guayaquil International Airport. Chris, who was the aircraft commander on this flight, decided to leave the plane fueled for the next day, so while he went to the base office to fill out some paper work, I began to prepare the airplane for the refueling, one of the copilot functions. When the fuel truck finally showed up, it was already dark and to top it off, the driver hadn't brought a ladder to reach the fuel tank openings on the top of the wing. So I had to get on top of the wing through the emergency hatch above the cockpit with a rope to pull the fuel hose up to the wing. In order to see well, I was using a pocket penlight. In an eye blink, the penlight slipped out of my hand and fell to the bottom of the fuel tank two and a half feet deep. Oh shit! Now I was in deep trouble.

I knew exactly what had to be done. I had to recover that flashlight; otherwise, the plane would be grounded. A foreign object of that size could obstruct the fuel flow from the tank to the pressure pump that feeds the engines. I forced my hand in the opening that was about four inches round and it entered, and I kept sliding my forearm until I got to my elbow. That was as far as it would go. After several minutes trying to force it in, I realized it wasn't going to go past my elbow joint.

Now what? The impatient truck driver had already asked me what the delay was to start dispensing the fuel. He needed to go to the other side of the runway to replenish other aircraft.

"Look, better you take care of the other airplanes. I have a problem with the tank lid. It's stuck and won't open," I told him in a calm, calculating voice.

He pulled down the hose spout, wound it up and left. When I heard the truck leave, I felt an instant relief without his presence pressuring me. I managed to get my arm out and soaked it with JP-4 fuel, which is an oily mixture of kerosene with gasoline, and tried again. I began to twist my arm from left to right as if prying a locked nut, and my elbow finally slipped through the opening, and I was able to grab the penlight on the bottom of the tank with my first and middle finger. I had the penlight pressed so hard that my fingers ached. I then began to slowly pull my arm out, but when it got to my elbow, it wouldn't go any farther. For a moment it crossed my mind to jerk my arm out with all my strength, but that would mean tearing my skin and probably fracturing my elbow in the process. I couldn't help but remember a novel I had read as a child where a wolf in his despair to free himself had gnawed his paw off when he got it caught in a trap. I tried hard not to panic. I took three deep breaths and began to evaluate my predicament. It had taken me over five minutes of arm twisting to get it to go in, so I took a deep breath and once again with renewed patience and determination decided to try once more, this time the opposite way. Finally, after much twisting and pulling and some pain, I got my arm out with the penlight still between my fingers. I sat on the wing exhausted and relieved. When I looked down at the penlight, I realized that at no moment had the penlight ceased to emit light! I closed the fuel cap and got off the wing. I didn't confide what had happened with anyone. I figured the matter was now behind me and there was no need to share my ordeal. One thing for sure was that I would not attempt to fuel an airplane in the dark ever again. Either it would be in the daytime or in a well-lit area, period. I dutifully wrote down that refueling episode in my little red book in the Never Again section. The important thing was that the flight wouldn't be cancelled because of my blunder. The next day, in bright daylight, the airplane was fueled, and the flight left on time.

That night at the hotel, after that frantic refueling incident, I slowly began to feel normal. I learned from the orders for the next day's mission that we were to take the US Embassy's military attaché to an Ecuadorian military outpost in the Amazon River basin. We were first to go to Shell Mera for fuel and from there fly to our final destination, Santiago. Shell Mera, had been the site of a Shell Oil Company camp since 1944 and later a Pan American Grace Airlines (Panagra) operations center. They had operated DC-2s and later DC-3s that covered the entire South American Pacific coast, including Panama. The airport now served as an Ecuadorian military base as well as the headquarters of Mission Aviation Fellowship (MAF). I was aware of the events involving MAF missionaries who had perished at the hands of members of the Huarorani ethnic group in 1955.[37-A] On a trip to the MAF headquarters in California to pick up and ferry a Dillon Construction, Ltd Cessna185 to Panama with Chris Dillon, I had visited an MAF memorial exhibition dedicated to the five members lost in that tragedy. An attempt by these missionaries to approach the Huaroranis resulted in confused versions of how the outcome unfolded but ended with the violent death of all five missionaries. The remarkable ending of this tragedy is that some of those who are attributed with the killings now serve as evangelizers in that same remote Ecuadorean region. Today, on the banks of the Curaray River, the site where this tragedy occurred is used for baptisms of the new converts.

The day dawned with a low cloud base that shielded the sun, but as the flight would be at an altitude of 19,000 feet, this shouldn't be an issue. We had to cross the Andes mountain range to the east to get to Shell Mera. As we climbed past 10,000 feet, we donned oxygen masks as per EHA operational procedures. We were in IMC, in dense puffy clouds, and at 15,000 feet the passengers were instructed to put on their oxygen masks as well. An hour into the flight, I happened to look down at my hands and saw that my fingernails were blue, a clear indication that I was not getting oxygen into my bloodstream, as I should. Something was not working with my oxygen bottle. Although I didn't feel euphoric, which is another one of the symptoms of hypoxia, I was a bit dizzy, and since I'd had previous experience with hypoxia, I immediately located another oxygen bottle and connected it to my mask. After a few minutes, I felt normal again, and I recalled Dorcey's bout with lack of oxygen years back while cloud seeding. At 17,000 feet we broke out to a clear blue sky with unlimited visibility. To our right was the Chimborazo volcano with its snow-covered peak, a breathtaking sight. We continued climbing and leveled at 19,000 feet. After a short while, we descended and landed in Shell Mera and fueled for our next leg. On the other side of the runway, the MAF offices were visible with their airplanes parked outside. They had not been deterred by the Curaray incident years back.

For the rest of the trip, we relied solely on our onboard GPS. Far from any navigational aids, we couldn't receive radio signals. We were flying low over a dense layer of jungle crisscrossed by a river that I assumed was the Curaray. The Santiago runway was a swath of asphalt located in the middle of that jungle. A reception committee led by an Ecuadorian colonel who had arrived in a Hughes 500 helicopter was there to receive our passengers. I had a general idea of where we were, but never imagined how close we were to the site where the Huarorani had first encountered the missionaries in 1956. After lunch, from the balcony of the officer's dining hall in full sight of the river, I asked an Ecuadorean officer about the infamous incident involving the five missionaries. Yes, it was the Curaray River, he asserted, but he had never heard of the incident that had stunned the world community at the time.

In this first week of flying for EHA, I had been to so many places of historical and political importance. Was this to be the norm from now on? Little did I know...

Chapter 38
Woes of the Captaincy

In those days SOUTHCOM hadn't yet required that both crewmembers be qualified as aircraft commanders, or captain as it's known in civilian aviation. So as expected, after I got my captaincy, I flew my first hours as a captain with an experienced copilot. Tony had been flying several years in the company, although I don't know why he hadn't been promoted to captain. He must have felt in his comfort zone, without the responsibilities of a pilot-in-command. Tony was experienced flying in Colombia and shared with me the peculiarities required to operate in certain places that weren't contemplated in the company's operations manual. I valued that and besides, we made a good team.

In a month or so, Tony resigned to go to fly in Peru and I was assigned another copilot who was completely the opposite. Although he executed takeoffs and landings and en route navigation satisfactorily, that was it. He didn't have the slightest idea, or worse yet, interest about flight preparation, execution, or termination. The first time we had to fly together, I coached him on the basics of the job, such as radio communication, flight plan preparation, weight and balance calculations, and weather reports interpretation. But there was no response. Nothing.

At first I thought he was just lazy, but after a few more flights, he demonstrated that he didn't have the minimum mental skills to be part of a flight crew. His lack of judgment and common sense was troublesome. During several flights he confirmed his lack of aptitude and reasoning, especially for the type of flying in unique areas such as where we flew. In all honesty, he was a burden on the flight deck. He didn't have a clue of situational awareness, no perception of what was going on around him. When one is moving, or things around you are moving, your perception requires periodic and valid updates. Often times those updates require only your ears and mind's eye in order to draw an accurate situational awareness picture, other times, such as when you're immersed inside a cloud, you have to rely on your airplane's instrumentation. In his case, he didn't have that awareness in either setting. Off the airplane, he also had much to desire as far as behavior. His conduct dealing with people was indecorous and obnoxious, especially with the opposite sex. He kept me on guard on the ground as well as in the air.

But the straw that broke the camel's back happened one morning while taking off from Bogota under IMC conditions. Departures from El Dorado Airport, especially in IMC, require being precise; not only for the heavy air traffic, but also because of the mountainous terrain that surrounds the airport. While on a departure procedure turn, and moments after requesting After Takeoff Check List, the navigation and communications equipment suddenly went blank. Holy shit! What happened?

I shifted my eyes to my right expecting to see the copilot scrutinizing the problem, since he was the Pilot Monitoring and should have been monitoring everything related to the flight while the other pilot, the Pilot Flying, concentrates on flying the airplane. But he was just sitting there calmly. He hadn't realized what had just happened. That was how naïve and unconnected his manner was.

As I kept my bank and climb, I checked the circuit breaker (CB) panel behind the copilot's seat to see if any had blown. All CBs were in order; none had blown. But when I scanned the top panel, I noticed the Avionics Master switch, which controls the entire electrical system of the aircraft's navigation and communication components, was in the OFF position. The copilot must have inadvertently flipped it off while performing the After Takeoff Checklist. I switched it back on again and in a few seconds got the electrical components back on-line. Then and there I made a decision to keep his hands off anything related to the flight. Furthermore, I didn't even allow him to transmit on the radio; his radio protocol was confusing, long and repetitive, so much so that on more than one occasion other crews sharing the same frequency made foul comments about his demeanor.

After flying a couple of days with me doing everything, I felt physically exhausted. I didn't only fly all the legs, but I took care of the seven checklists, handled the tower, control center, and Davis-Monthan communications, supervised the cargo loading and re-fueling; in addition to the captain's responsibility which included: formulating the risk assessment for each flight, interpreting the weather reports, calculating the weight and balance, determining routes, altitudes, fuel consumption and preparing the flight plans and, at the end of the day, filling the endless after-flight reports. It was exhausting, yes, but I was determined not to let this absent-minded copilot interfere with the flights. I counted the days to return to Panama and culminate this nine-day assignment that seemed never ending.

On the morning we were to fly back to Panama, while we were waiting for the embassy van to take us to the airport, I noticed the copilot lugging a large cardboard box that hadn't been part of his baggage when we arrived. I immediately asked him what it contained, and he replied that he thought they were ceramic pieces and that he was doing his girlfriend's brother in Bogota a favor by brining it to her to Panama.

"What? You think it contains ceramics but you don't know for sure? No way is that crap getting on the airplane! We're not in Columbia, South Carolina; we're in Colombia, South America!"

A hotel security guard, who had been witnessing the scene, called me aside: "*Mire, Capitán*, it's not the first time that this gentleman carries packages to Panama for others. Strange people, I tell you, but you've been the only one who's said or done anything about it. We have orders from management not to get involved, but I tell you, they're shady people."

The van arrived, we boarded and the cardboard box stayed on the sidewalk in front of the hotel. The security guards had their orders not to get near it.

Although the destination was Panama, we had to make a stopover in Barranquilla at a naval base inside the Ernesto Cortissoz Airport compound. We were programmed to refuel and pick up some passengers before continuing to Panama. In Colombia, EHA flights were considered diplomatic flights since they were managed through the US Embassy so we were given special treatment. They didn't check the plane, cargo, baggage or crew. But that day when we arrived at the base, as soon as we landed, the narcotics dogs went through our entire luggage while the military personnel checked the plane. I viewed all this with some skepticism, and it wasn't until the dogs and anti-narcotics agents had left that I felt somewhat at ease.

There was no fuel on base, so we had to taxi the plane to the civilian terminal to refuel. When we arrived there, this time the airport security civil component climbed onboard to check our baggage. I was fuming, not at the security people, but at the copilot's stupidity and naivety in accepting to bring a parcel without knowing what was in it. The return flight was one of total sterile cabin, just like the previous days, but even more intense on my part. As soon we landed in Panama, I requested a meeting with the operations manager. I explained the incident just experienced, in addition to several other highly compromising situations that convinced me that this copilot was a threat to the operation. I emphatically refused to fly with him anymore. A meeting with the other captains was called for the next day to evaluate my complaint. In that meeting the other captains in unison agreed that this copilot was not only a hindrance in the cockpit, but a threat.

I asked disbelievingly why they hadn't spoken out. One of them replied: "I just don't let him touch anything on the plane during the flight. I ignore him." A conference call was placed to the Anchorage Director of Operations, who, upon hearing the complaint, immediately ordered he be let go in situ. He was fired on the spot.

Weeks later when I returned to that same hotel in Bogota, the security guard who had had been present during the cardboard box incident narrated to me that the box had remained on the sidewalk all that day in front of the hotel. They had followed management's strict orders to steer clear of it. He affirmed that most likely the *Pepenadores*, entire families who comb the Bogota business center streets at night on horse-pulled carts collecting recyclable material to sell, had taken the cardboard box away.

"If they did, then they hit the jackpot," he said, implying that what was inside the ceramic figurines was illicit drugs with a high black market value. A modus operandi of drug traffickers, he went on to tell me, was sending one or two "dummy loads" with a third party, unaware or not of its contents; if the parcel manages to pass the customs scrutiny without being detected, the next ones are sure to be "impregnated."

Had I not been skeptical, it's likely that I would still be locked up in a Colombian prison for drug trafficking, because on the ground or in flight, the person responsible for the aircraft is the PIC, not the company, not the cargo agent, and for sure not the copilot. It's the captain commanding the flight, period. Months later, after this copilot had left, we found out he had gotten a job in a US military base in the Middle East as a civilian flight instructor. How he ever managed to coax these people into hiring him, I'll never know, but then, he had also managed it with EHA.

Chapter 39
Mexican Stopover

I got an assignment to ferry a Casa 212 from Panama to Marana, Arizona, Evergreen's headquarters for major repairs for a routine structural inspection. Once there, I would fly another recently re-conditioned Casa 212 back to Panama. The flight took two days in a hellish heat; the Casa is not a comfortable airplane and besides, it has no on board air conditioning. We spent the night in Veracruz and continued the next day to Marana. I had a routine route check pending, so Hayden, EHA check airman from Anchorage, accompanied me on that flight as copilot and to give me a check ride on this flight. It was the longest check ride ever, since every possible emergency or mechanical in-flight failure was simulated, mainly to break the tediousness of that long flight. It seems all the questions from the airplane's flight manual were asked. It was definitely not a pleasure flight, but I enjoyed it to the fullest.

Marana Airport is located on a dry desert and for that reason contains the largest transport aircraft storage in the world. Thousands of all makes and models of airplanes are parked as if waiting to fly again. Most likely, they won't, but parts and equipment may be reclaimed for other aircraft. A few miles farther down the road, next to Davis-Monthan Air Base, a large number of military combat and transport aircraft are also waiting to be reactivated for service. During the Vietnam War, many Second World War fighters and bombers were reconditioned back to flying status. On the one hand it is impressive to see all array of aircraft with their respective logos painted on the fuselage, but on the other it's disheartening to know that most of these veteran aircraft will never fly again. One aircraft I didn't see was a DC-3/C-47!

Two days after we arrived, we received the Casa 212 that we were to fly back to Panama. After an acceptance flight, we refueled and began our journey south. My crew consisted of JB[39-A] as copilot and a mechanic from the Panama base. JB had joined EHA after retiring from flying for the US Army. He was captain in EHA's Beechcraft 1900 and was assigned on this flight to familiarize him in the Casa, as EHA wanted to have their captains who were assigned to Panama checked out in those two airplanes.

The first overnight we chose was Acapulco, Mexico. After dinner at the hotel, we swung by the lobby to watch a Karaoke competition. Aware of the FAA's ten hours regulation on drinking alcoholic beverages before a flight, and EHA's twelve hours "Bottle to Throttle," as it is commonly referred to, at ten o'clock that night I bade goodbye and reminded the two crewmembers of the next day's early flight.

The next morning when the mechanic didn't appear for breakfast and didn't answer the phone, I went to his room. There was no sign that he had slept in the bed. This was unusually strange and disturbing so JB and I decided to report to the hotel administration. After sending helpers to search the hotel's surrounding area, the visibly nervous manager decided to call the police, then the hospitals, and at the end, even the morgue. After an hour, a police lieutenant arrived, and the first thing he told us after hearing us out was that it was usual for tourists to go missing after a night on the town, and that most likely he had gotten enthusiastic over some *chamaquita*. I didn't readily accept that cavalier theory, so I proceeded to talk to the security guard who was still on duty from the night before. Nobody knew anything. The hotel was in a huge complex of hotels, restaurants and nightclubs that catered to the guests and selected locals. The entrance to the premises was restricted for the safety of the guests. According to JB, he and the mechanic had crossed the street to a Hard Rock Cafe, and the last time he saw him was at midnight when they were leaving and the mechanic stopped to talk to some women outside the parking lot.

"*Ahí está.* He fell in love! He'll show up any minute now. You'll see," said the lieutenant as he got into his patrol car to leave. "Closed case."

I knew that our missing crewmember was aware of our early planned departure, and though not bound by the 12-hour alcohol-free rule for pilots, he was a dependable person.

We crossed the street to the Hard Rock Cafe to find information on our lost mechanic's whereabouts. We sent for the security guard who was also on duty the night before and when I described him, right away he said he remembered seeing him get in a taxi with two women and a man wearing a Black Jaguar Nightclub T-shirt. The manager, who recognized the name of the club, drove us in his car to a neighborhood full of cantinas and nightclubs in the center of Acapulco. Sure enough, we found our AWOL friend in The Black Jaguar, sitting in the middle of a mixed group of men and women. The atmosphere was festive, but he seemed to be in a stupor, more asleep than awake. He spoke incoherently and didn't recognize either of us when we forcibly lugged him out of the club to the car. This search and rescue operation took a large part of the day, and it wasn't until the afternoon that we were able to take off for Liberia, Costa Rica, by the way of Tapachula, Mexico.

During the flight to Liberia, JB and I discussed what had happened and the problem and scare that our now not-too-favorite mechanic had caused. However, we were relieved that it hadn't turned out worse. Abeam the Guatemalan coast, the radar painted a line of bad weather that extended from the mountain range to our left, to well inside the Pacific Ocean. We couldn't climb over it because the tops were showing on the radar to be over 23,000 feet, which was more than the Casa 212's absolute ceiling. There was no other way than to penetrate the weather at the narrowest part. The turbulence would be severe. Since the cabin was in a cargo configuration with no seats, our rescued friend was asleep on the floor with his backpack as a pillow. JB tried to wake him up so he could come to the cockpit where there was an observer seat with a seatbelt, but he wouldn't budge. The man was knocked out. With all the tumbles and swaying from the turbulence, he never flinched. He rolled from side to side and at times was suspended in the air before dropping hard on the deck. The impacts didn't seem to faze him. When we finally landed in Liberia at 9 o'clock at night after a very long and stressful day, he was still groggy and had to be helped getting into a taxi and into his hotel room.

The next day at breakfast, we confronted him on what had happened. He claimed he only remembered talking with a group of ladies after leaving the club and nothing else after that. After that description of events, JB and I, since we both had attended the narcotics talk required of EHA crew operating in Colombia, quickly deduced that he had probably been drugged with Scopolamine.[39-B] Once convinced of this possibility, our hard feelings toward him dissipated.

Back in Panama days later, our mechanic, now recovered, told us that when he returned home, he discovered that his two credit cards had been depleted in five different ATM's in Acapulco that night. Besides being drugged, he had been taken on a *Cajero Express* tour, a common hijack/scam in the nightlife world. What his excuse for that night's loss of their savings to his wife was, we never found out, but it must have been interesting to hear. For us, it had been a lesson to learn from our now esteemed mechanic's mistake.

Chapter 40
Mission Rejected

Two years after flying for EHA, unexpectedly we were required to attend a talk by a member of embassy's Military Group (MILGROUP) in Bogota. The conference entailed procedures to be followed in case of being apprehended or captured if forced to make a jungle landing or if kidnapped in the city. The four stages consisted of: Captivity, Evasion, Resistance, and Escape (CERE). Why were we being briefed on this now? What did the MILGROUP know that we didn't? When asked, we weren't told the reason, but we had noticed a marked increase in operations related to rescuing the three Americans held in captivity by the FARC.[40-A]

While we operated in areas considered dangerous, to my knowledge we were never exposed unnecessarily. Each flight had to be approved from the Davis-Monthan Air Base Commander who received confirmation from the US Embassy in Bogota about the presence of the Colombian military authorities at our destinations of that day.

I believe that the CERE briefing we got that night had to do with an abnormal mission we were briefed on by another member of the MILGROUP a few weeks later. This person met us at the ramp one night as we were getting out of our plane and requested an important meeting prior to our ride to the hotel. That night Chris, although a captain himself, was my copilot. We had been flying all day and here we were, just debarking from the plane on a dark, rainy night, hungry and just wanting to get to the hotel to shower and dine, and this person wants to have a meeting? We reluctantly accepted. He got to the point at once, letting us know that we would be doing night flights, at low altitude over the ground, dropping flyers in areas of "interest." When we asked what the leaflets contained, he disclosed that they offered monetary rewards to those who gave information on the whereabouts of three abducted Americans held by the FARC.

"And why at low altitude and at night?" I asked.

"Because if the flyers are dropped from too high, they won't reach their objective, and if they're dropped during the day, you might attract small arms fire."

"Wait a moment. Why don't you use the Colombian Air Force for this operation?"

"There's still no consensus between the Police, the Army and the Air Force. The time is now, for strategic reasons that we cannot divulge to you at this time."

Chris and I looked at each other, got up, grabbed our flight bags and left the office to board the van back to the hotel. As far as I was concerned, my EHA contract didn't specify night flights at low altitude and much less being exposed to small arms fire. That was the last time we heard of that proposal.

Weeks after this meeting, the rescue of the three Americans, various Colombian military and police members and of some civilians successfully took place.

Chapter 41
End of a Saga

My logbook records that on March 25, 2009, we had taken off at ten-thirty in the morning from Bogota to Tumaco on the Pacific coast near the border with Ecuador. It was a routine flight and consisted of picking up a contingent of Colombian and US Special Forces soldiers, who had been on patrol in the jungle, and returning them to CATAM in Bogota. My copilot that day was Brad.[41-A]

We had left Bogota under dark clouds and rain, but the weather in Tumaco was sunny and bright. It was nice to feel the sun's warmth after Bogota's cold and damp climate. Tumaco is a port that's grown progressively, but at the same time, it's also become an important stepping-stone for drug trafficking, and all the mayhem that comes with that.

When we got back to the airport from our lunch in town, I heard someone calling out: "Ibu, Ibu!" It was Mike, a DynCorp mechanic/pilot. DynCorp was contracted by Plan Colombia to help eradicate coca crops in Colombia. They operated Air Tractor 502-B and Vietnam War era twin-engine Bronco (North American OV-10) aircraft for this aerial application operation. I knew Mike from his days in Panama when he had worked at Howard AFB and we had cultivated a friendship through flying and airplanes. Aviation was the common bond. Mike invited us to his office and then gave us a tour of the complex. In the back yard, we came across a beached narco-submarine captured by the Colombian naval forces. It was typical of those used to transport cocaine from the Colombian coasts to Central America and Mexico.[41-B] It was one of the first designs that came out several years ago. The later designs were much more sophisticated to the point that in 2006 one reached the Spanish coast. It had crossed the Atlantic Ocean loaded with cocaine.

It was nearly nightfall when our passengers showed up with all their gear and equipment. The airport would be closed in ten minutes, one hour after sunset. Without facilities to weigh the passengers and their equipment, I assigned a standard weight of 200 pounds per person plus gear. The Casa 212 was configured to accommodate 27 people plus cargo for that flight. They were in total 28 so one of them had to sit in the observer seat in between us pilots. Holy shit! What a big mistake that was! The Casa was heavy, but since Tumaco was at sea level and at this hour the temperature had decreased, the weight and balance calculations indicated that we were within the limit for takeoff. We managed to leave just minutes before the authorities closed the airport because of the time. As soon as the wheels left the ground, our passengers whooped and hollered. I could understand why. They would sleep in beds with clean sheets, bathe with clean fresh water and eat hot meals. They acted like little kids on a field trip. But up front in the cockpit, we were nauseated from the combined ripe smell of our guest in the jump seat and the putrid odor that emanated from behind in the cabin. They had been patrolling in the jungle for thirty days. We understood and sympathized, but that didn't make the air any less stifling.

Hours earlier a device had exploded in the docks area, and Tumaco had automatically been declared a "hot zone." In those cases, our operating procedures indicated that altitude be gained as quickly over the ocean before heading towards the western mountain range that had to be crossed at 17,000 feet. The Casa's two Garrett turbo-prop engines developed maximum performance and climbed steadily towards our final altitude. When passing through 8,000 feet in a non-pressurized airplane, the internal pressure of the body is greater than that of the air that surrounds it, causing the body's natural gases to seek to escape. Well, in a short time as we climbed, the foul smell of the passengers' gases mixed with those of their unwashed bodies and clothes became unbearable. It was just too much. As a rule, the crew must don their oxygen mask when passing through 10,000 feet. But in this case, this particular crew put on our masks right away, no matter how uncomfortable they might be. We were attempting to block off the strong smells, but they persisted, mask or no mask. The other solution that occurred to me was to partially open the hydraulic rear-loading ramp to suck out all that bad smell. Sure enough, once we opened a crack on the ramp the problem was solved, but it made the inside of the plane intensely cold. The Casa's heating system is terrible. The hot air from the engines enters the cabin through the floor vents under the pilot's feet with no possibility to control it; so to avoid burning their feet, the crews don't use it. As we continued to climb to 17,000 feet, the air inside the cabin reached freezing temperatures. Even so, we found it was better to freeze than to be subjected to the awful smell from our passengers.

We arrived to a dark, cold Bogota with its characteristic drizzle, frozen to the bone and with a planeload of sleeping passengers; over half of them were already asleep when we passed through 15,000 feet, the altitude where the passengers are required to be using oxygen. Most of them had not donned their masks. Once the door opened to disembark, they woke up and the laughter and the racket picked up again. After saying our goodbyes, I don't know if I felt happy for having fulfilled our duty by bringing them back to civilization, or to see them drive away in the dreadful stench that emanated from the bus that transported them.

That flight would be my second to last with Evergreen. The next day, on March 26, when we arrived at the airport for a flight to San Jose del Guaviare, we learned that all EHA flights in Colombia had been canceled. Our directive was to proceed immediately to Panama, where we were informed that the contract with SOUTHCOM had come to an end. Word had it that since the main objective of the contract had been to support the effort to rescue the three Americans kidnapped by the FARC had been fulfilled, EHA's services were no longer needed.

Just as EHA ceased operations based in Panama, the DoD notified me that my security clearance was rejected because I had been on the payroll of a foreign government, Panama, when I worked in the ACP. It took them three and a half years to reach this conclusion.

In November, eight months after being unemployed by EHA, I received an offer from them to ferry a Casa from Anchorage to Kabul, Afghanistan, through parts of Russia, China and Mongolia. Initially the offer triggered my gypsy genes, but after analyzing the route, the time of year, and my lack of experience flying in subarctic regions, I declined. Months later, I found out from the crew that ferried the plane on that trip that it was a hellish ordeal full of unexpected horrific surprises. Instead of five days, it took twenty-five due to bad weather, mechanical problems, lack of spare parts and the perennial customs and immigration setbacks. I had made the right decision declining after all.

Several pilots continued to fly either with Evergreen or other contractors in different parts of the world, such as in Africa, and two of them got jobs flying with Copa Airlines in Panama. As for me, I had drained my desire for adventure. At least that's what I believed at that moment.

Above: The Casa 212-200, one of four operated by *Evergreen Helicopters of Alaska*, a subsidiary of *Evergreen International Aviation* from its base in Panama.

Below: Cockpit of the Casa 212-200, an office with a panoramic view.

Above: Submersible cabin utilized in the Dunking course. Lafayette, Louisiana, USA.

Below: Ibu and Tony. Uniform? What uniform? Cockpit of the Casa 212-200.

Above: Mike next to a narco-submarine captured in Tumaco, Nariño, Colombia.

Right: The Casa 212-200 in flight.

Below: A Globemaster C-17 "Ballena" (Whale) on take-off. Larandia, Caqueta, Colombia.

Part 9
Adrenaline Overdose

42 *Allure of Adventure*
43 *Unexpected Layover*
44 *Puerto Leguizamo*
45 *Jungle Haven*
46 *Acceptance and Determination*
47 *Distorted New Year*
48 *End of a Nightmare*

Chapter 42
Allure of Adventure

In December 2012, after I had stopped flying for EHA, we had moved to Boquete and had settled into a small community life style. I had brought both my 1955 Cessna 170B and my 1951 Cessna 140A from Panama City to David and flew mostly for myself and sporadically gave introductory flights for wannabe pilots.

The Mooney M20L had already been several days at Enrique Malek Airport in David waiting for parts to repair it. The plane had stopped in David on a flight from the US to Argentina with a US pilot and Jose Alomar, the Argentine mechanic, but en route to Panama City they had oil pressure problems and had to return to Malek. That was all I knew about the plane. I was allowing Jose to use my hangar facilities and tools for the repairs. A few days later the owner, Leandro Argentini, arrived ready to fly the plane out once it was repaired. The ferry pilot who had flown the plane to Panama had returned to the US and was no longer available for the flight. Since the aircraft was registered in the US (N158MP), but it was operating over Panamanian airspace, the Panamanian Civil Aviation Authority in compliance with International Civil Aeronautics Organization (ICAO) regulations prohibited the aircraft to fly over national airspace unless a Panamanian or US licensed pilot was PIC. The same would apply in Colombia, Brazil, and Bolivia, the three remaining countries that had to be flown over to get to Argentina. Either the PIC had a pilot license from the country of the over-flight or a pilot's license from the plane's country of registration, and Leandro had neither a Panamanian nor a US license, so he had to contract a pilot with an FAA license to fly the plane to Argentina.

When Leandro found out that I had a valid FAA license, he approached me about flying the Mooney to Argentina. The previous day he had made a test flight with another pilot who was also FAA licensed, but for reasons I don't know, Leandro proposed I make the trip with them. I thought about it for a few hours considering the date, the closeness of the end of the year, the route and the airplane's known previous mechanical conditions. I decided to make the trip mainly out of solidarity with them: trapped in a strange country with no clear way out. On one occasion in Mexico, I had found myself in a similar situation and was given a helping hand, so I think that gave me the justification I was looking for. Besides, I would be flying in unexplored territory for me, Brazil, Bolivia and Argentina, and that sparked up my latent adventurous spirit.

That afternoon we test flew the airplane. Right away I could tell Leandro had a natural ability to fly. But when we found scattered clusters of clouds at 3,000 feet, I noticed he became uncomfortable. I asked him about it, and he said that he was not instrument rated nor used to flying around the vicinity of heavy cloud; in Argentina, he usually flew under controlled airspace that starts at 1,500 feet. I suggested that he continue to climb avoiding the clouds as we were on a VFR flight. We made several maneuvers and tested the navigation equipment including an autopilot, and everything functioned normally. The Mooney was a pleasure to fly, responsive in controls and with an impressive powerful engine. This model in particular had a water-cooled 351 horsepower experimental engine. It could reach a cruising speed of more than 200 knots, faster than the turbo prop transport aircraft that I had flown in Aero Perlas or Evergreen. I decided I'd accompany them on the flight on the condition that the flight from David to Gelabert Airport in Panama City would be considered a test on the engine condition. If everything went well in that hour and a half flight, we would continue as planned to Bahia Blanca, Argentina.

Day 1- On December 28, although we had initiated the procedures for the departure from David in advance, last minute inconveniences that are never lacking in this type of flight slowed us down. In this case, AAC approval of the internal flight was required and 24 hours later they had not responded yet. I made a personal call to the AAC in Panama City and talked to contacts to help in complying with the requested permission for the flight. It was after midday when we finally got the authorization and managed to leave. Our VFR flight plan was for 9,500 feet in typical cloud conditions for that time of year. Leandro was flying while I familiarized myself with the sophisticated, for me, navigation instruments aboard. As we were flying near clouds, I again noticed Leandro's discomfort, so I radioed Panama Flight Center and requested an IFR authorization for the remainder of the flight to provide Leandro basic IMC flight instruction. His enthusiasm for flying and his ease in assimilating the basic IFR rules made the training session easy and enjoyable. The Mooney was well equipped to fly in IMC conditions: an automatic pilot, two VORs, two GPS units and also an ADF; though considered obsolete, the ADF is a useful aid when flying over isolated areas such as the ones on our flight plan. Leandro had the tendency to revert to the autopilot when we were inside a cloud, but I insisted he fly manually to get to know the airplane.

"Learn how to feel the plane first, then you can use the autopilot as many times as you like." I cautioned more than once.

Both Leandro and Jose had been stranded in David for several weeks and were overjoyed that they were finally in the air and back on the way to their home base in Argentina. They were treated to a unique sight of seeing both the Pacific and Atlantic Oceans at the same time, and when the Panama Canal with the city in the background came into view, they were euphoric. They were happy to be going home.

On the flight to Gelabert the engine worked fine. When we landed, as part of the exit requirements, I filled out the required flight plan as the PIC, and I sent Jose to fill the portable oxygen tank. This aircraft was not pressurized, and we would be flying at altitudes greater than 12,000 feet. I requested navigation charts of the route to follow and approach charts for the airports where we would land since there were none on board, but I only managed to get instrument approach charts at the Alfonso Bonilla Aragon Airport in Cali, Colombia, our first stop on this long trip. With the departure paperwork completed, we left Gelabert at three in the afternoon on an IFR clearance flying on the A321 airway that would keep us over the water almost all the way to Cali. The minimum en route altitude (MEA) was 3,000 feet, but I filed for 11,000 and once we passed the Perlas Archipelago, I requested a route deviation to fly 30 miles off the coast. Even though this change would make our flight path longer, it was the calculated distance and altitude in which the Mooney could glide to land in case of engine failure. Bob Deimert's lesson from years back had become firmly engraved in my way of flying over water.

The engine again worked normally on this three-hour leg, a relief to all of us. We arrived in Cali in the late afternoon where we refueled and checked the oil; all was well, it hadn't consumed any oil at all. Harry, the Aero Support representative that was attending our flight, drove us to a hotel in downtown Cali, but not before getting me an IFR approach chart for the Leticia airport in Colombia. I had wanted the chart for Tabatinga, Brazil, but since Leticia was across the river from Tabatinga, the Leticia one would do in a pinch. Little did I know then how lucky it was to have gotten that approach plate.

That night, the renowned Cali Fair was being inaugurated, and the receptionist suggested we check out the programmed activities, which were varied and inviting. This spiked our interest, as we were in a festive mood. The accomplishment of the flight that day gave us reason to celebrate. I hurried to get ready, but as I was leaving my room, I stopped and reassessed what I was about to do. My eagerness had overcome my fatigue, a product of the stress of flying several hours in a single-engine airplane over water. The next morning's flight over high mountains and desolate and remote areas would not be stress-free either. Then and there I decided to stay in my room and prepare for the flight the next day. I cancelled the planned city excursion, much to my travel mates' disappointment.

Without updated navigation charts for the remaining leg, I had to use the date-expired charts I had brought from my hangar in David, and they were helpful in preparing for the flight. The route would take us from Cali to Tabatinga, Brazil. We would have to climb and cross the Andes at 19,000 feet, the MEA for that route and fly several hours over the Amazon jungle, a desolate and soulless expanse. The next day I came to realize how prudent it was to have studied the route and to have gone to bed early and awakened with a clear mind and a rested body.

Chapter 43
Unexpected Layover

Day 2- On Saturday, December 29, we woke up to a fresh and cool morning and a sky partially covered in clouds. After breakfast, Harry picked us up at the agreed time to drive us to the airport and assist us with Immigration and Customs. Once at the Meteorology and Operations offices to present our flight plan, we got the destination and en route forecast report; not too bad, not too good: storms in the afternoon in the Leticia area. The Airway selected would put us between the Western and Central mountain ranges, towards the colonial city of Popayan and then we would head eastwards. The mountains we were to cross are part of the Andes mountain range that extends from the Colombian Caribbean to the Chilean-Argentine Pacific coasts. Once on the east side of the mountain range we would be flying over the Caqueta plains and the Putumayo and Amazonia jungles and over to Leticia, located on the Amazon River and border point for Colombia, Peru and Brazil. Just across the Amazon River, lay Tabatinga, Brazil, our destination. Since we were estimating our arrival at Tabatinga at noon, the predicted storms didn't concern us much.

The normalized departure for aircraft taking off from the Cali airport on runway 01, (010° Magnetic) but heading in a southerly direction, requires a rapid climb, turning south right after takeoff to cross the VOR at the south end of the runway at 6,000 feet. Considering the speed of the Mooney, this requires that the ascent be 1,500 feet per minute, and to comply, the engine controls are set to maximum power. We check over the VOR at the indicated altitude and will continue climbing to reach the 19,000 feet assigned to this route. Once over the Popayan VOR, we will cross the mountains to our left. As we climb at full power the sky is overcast with mid-level cumulus clouds that look like harmless cotton balls, but I know they are consistently accompanied with severe turbulence. They're at different levels and obstruct the visibility on our route. We have to fly through them as we're on an IFR flight plan and shouldn't leave our assigned path without authorization, something I don't intend to do. Even though we can't see them, we're climbing between two mountain ranges.

As we pass 12,000 feet heading to the Popayan VOR, I ask Jose to prepare the oxygen, and that's when I find out the bottle is one-third full. It wasn't filled either in Panama or in Cali. What? Shit! This can't be happening! I had asked Jose to take care of the oxygen before we left Gelabert in Panama. I advise them both to hook up to the oxygen bottle and to refrain from any unnecessary talk in order not to consume what little oxygen we have in the bottle too quickly. We're now passing 15,000 feet, the altitude I know is my maximum tolerance without oxygen so I connect my mask to the bottle. As we pass 16,500 Jose beckons me with one hand and slides the other across his throat to indicate that we've run out of oxygen. *Mierda, carajo!*

Unexpectedly we break out on top of the clouds and have a gorgeous panorama in front of us. In the distance to the left we could see the Nevado de Huila mountain peak with its snow-capped summit that reaches up to 17,683 feet, and beyond that a completely clear green plateau. This gives me some relief. Being in visual conditions and below the Positive Control Airspace, which is 18,000 feet and cognizant of the terrain, I immediately request Cali Control Center to cancel IFR. We'll continue on a VFR flight plan. This means changing from restricted flying under the monitoring of the Control Center to a flight in visual conditions, allowing us to vary routes and altitudes, as long as we have visual contact with the ground. The controller asks if we're familiar with the area and my answer is yes.

"*Mantenga pleno contacto con el terreno*," he advises us. He then gives us the frequency to contact once we cross the mountains. Almost directly below us we see the small town of La Plata, a reference point where we'll turn left towards the east until crossing El Carmen, another village that's used as reference in visual flights, on the other side of the range. This crossing can be safely done at 15,500, as long as we're visual, and have full contact with the ground.

We cross over a ravine at 1,000 feet below, keeping our eyes on the steep slopes rising vertically on both sides. Once on the other side, on the east side, we quickly start a descent to 11,500 feet, since we have already been several minutes without breathing pure oxygen. From now on we don't have to fly at high altitudes; what's ahead, until we reach Bolivia at least, is flat jungle with no protruding obstacles. The engine has performed normally in terms of oil pressure and temperature, fuel flow, cylinder head temperature and manifold pressure, in addition to the most sensitive indicators for a pilot, its vibration that the pilot feels on his rear. These last indicators have been both even and constant. We level at 11,500 and cross over Florencia Airport, and then Larandia, a Colombian military outpost that I visited often when flying with EHA. I make a mental note that we're now flying over territory considered hostile. It was here that in March 2002, the FARC guerrilla group kidnapped Ingrid Betancourt and her assistant, Clara Rojas, while campaigning for the Colombian presidential elections. Then, the next year, on February 13, 2003, the FARC captured three Plan Colombia US civilians when their single-engine Caravan C-207 crashed landed during a power failure.

A lot of memories fill my mind related to those flights in this region, mostly good, but sprinkled with some I could have done without. A call from the Larandia Tower asking for position, altitude and time en route to the next reporting point quickly brings me back to reality. We give our estimate to the next reporting point that will be the Tres Esquinas VOR, located on the Colombian Air Force base, Colonel Ernesto Esguerra, near the Colombian-Ecuadorian border in Putumayo. Flying to the southeast, we have the morning sun almost in front of us, but the conditions are severe visual with few cumulus clouds below us. As we fly over the Puerto Leguizamo VOR, since there's no control tower at Caucaya, the Puerto Leguizamo airport, we report our position to the Tres Esquinas Tower.

I feel comfortable and enthusiastic because soon we will be flying over part of the Colombian Amazon region that I never did get to see. Years before I had read *A Story with Wings*, by the German-Colombian aviation pioneer, Herbert Boy, and I was captivated. In these memoirs, Boy recounts his air experiences during the Colombian-Peruvian War in the 1930s. My excitement overflows and I eagerly try to spot Puerto Boy, which was named in his honor. I know it must be somewhere below us on the banks of the Orteguaza River. I recognize the river by its chocolate colored water meandering stealthily through the jungle, but I can't locate Puerto Boy. I should have obtained the geographic coordinates when I could have, but instead of regrets, I focus on the immense beauty of the jungle below.

Tres Esquinas controller passes us to Villavicencio Control. We try to communicate but are unable to contact them, so we request a Colombian Air Force airplane on our same frequency to relay our position and ETA over our next reporting position, which is the Rolus fix. Good. Now that's done. In a few more hours we should be landing in Tabatinga. *Todo bien!*

Mentally I begin to practice the few phrases of Brazilian Portuguese that I know. We're all relaxed and chatting trivialities, especially the Argentines. Leandro talks about the reception they have planned on the family's Bahia Blanca ranch, which will have a pampero-style barbecue and Jose of the *maté* that he'll drink when he arrives in his homeland. He's been away over a month trying to get the Mooney to Argentina. All of a sudden, they alert me to the oil pressure gauge oscillation. I can't understand their reason for the alarm. The needle is visibly between the green and yellow markings, and that's in the normal range.

"What's the problem? The needle is in range." I ask and affirm with a certain air of knowledge.

"It's the oscillation!" Both tell me simultaneously. While they argue about the significance or not of this anomaly, I pull out my obsolete charts from my hanger in David to see if I locate our position. The Peruvian border is on the right but that's definitely out of consideration. An incursion into Peruvian territory would cause us great problems. In Cali, Harry had insisted that under no circumstances should we fly over Peruvian territory. Peruvians have a track record of shooting down unidentified aircraft first and asking questions later. So the only option is to return to Puerto Leguizamo, which we left eighty-five nautical miles behind.

"Go back to Puerto Leguizamo!" I tell Leandro, who is flying. "Make a 180° turn now!"

They continue to discuss the cause of the oscillation, but at that moment I'm not interested in the cause. It could be that cavitation is taking place; the oil pressure pump sucks air from an empty reservoir. Without oil, zero lubrication, without lubrication, the engine seizes and stops!

I warn Leandro to maintain altitude. In these cases it's vital to have altitude for a greater glide range if a forced landing is imminent. The Putumayo River is now on our left, but you can't see any boats or towns on any of the riverbanks. About ten miles from Puerto Leguizamo, we start the descent to try to locate the runway, which I remember being about five miles from the VOR. We locate it and begin our approach. With no control tower, we announce our intentions transmitting in the blind just in case there are other aircraft operating in the area. We quickly land and once on the ground, we turn off the engine and let the airplane continue to roll until it stops at mid runway. The three of us sit without making any move to exit. After a few moments we react and leave the cabin. We push the Mooney to the ramp in front of a shoddy tin-roofed building that serves as a terminal. The few persons at the airport just look and stare at what we're doing.

The first thing we do is check the oil content. There are only four quarts of oil left, which means we have lost eight quarts since we left Cali a few hours earlier this morning, an abnormally high consumption. Now I'm interested in knowing why. On our hands and knees we check the plane's underside and there is oil all over it, a clear sign that the oil loss was through the engine's vent tube. Jose is sure too much pressure in the reservoir forced the oil out through the vent tube.

"Well, I accept the theory," I answer, "but why this high pressure in the reservoir?"

"It must be that one or more cylinders are losing compression through the piston rings, increasing the pressure in the reservoir and forcing the oil through the vent tube," says Jose, convinced he's right.

For now we're stranded in a place without any mechanical services in sight, without adequate tools or appropriate instrumentation to confirm or disprove Jose's theory. A group of curious persons has already gathered around but when the police arrive, they disperse. One person remains, Miguel. He offers to assist us in whatever he can. At that point, I couldn't have imagined the crucial role Miguel's presence would play on this trip.

Jose proposes that in order to limit the amount of oil loss, we should cut off five inches of the end of the tube located inside the oil reservoir so that not so much oil is sucked into the engine case. I'm extremely skeptical about this solution, but at the convincing insistence of the two, I reluctantly agree. Even though in the official documentation I appear as pilot in command, in reality my presence is due to my FAA license, which legalizes this flight. Leandro is the owner and Jose the mechanic, and this fact makes me feel that their inputs and thoughts carry some weight. Up to a certain point. While we're pondering the idea of cutting the tube, Miguel shows up on his motorbike with a person who has a few tools in a cloth bag strung across his shoulder. We had asked Miguel if there were any mechanics in town with tools, and this is what we got. Immediately Leandro and Jose get involved in the task of removing the vent tube, while I deal with the police authorities to explain our unannounced arrival.

After several hours of toiling, improvising, modifying and retooling some of the borrowed wrenches, the tube is finally removed and Leandro jumps on the motorbike with Miguel and heads to town to have the tube shortened by five inches. They return a few minutes later, and the installation takes less time than the removal, but between that and getting lubricating oil and fuel, both automotive since there are no aviation products in Puerto Leguizamo, sunset suddenly is announcing its arrival. We manage to make a fifteen-minute test flight and check for possible leaks once we land. None, the belly is clean and there are no apparent oil leaks, and none of the original 12 quarts seems to have been spent. It seems that the fidgeting will work after all. The trip is programmed for the next day. The police assign us a patrol that accompanies us at all times, whether to search for a hotel, to dine and even to walk through the town square. I'm not sure if it's for our protection or because they just want to keep an eye on us, not knowing exactly if we are who we say we are: three stranded foreigners on the way to Argentina. However, they are cordial and helpful in every way.

We find lodgings in Hotel Cano in the center of town. After getting settled and cleaned up, the first thing we do is try to communicate with Harry in Cali to inform him of our predicament and to warn the aviation authorities what's happened in order to avoid a search being initiated since they must already have information that we never arrived at Tabatinga at the estimated time. The police escort accompanies us to a restaurant and stand watch outside as we dine and even offer us a tour of the town nightlife, which we reluctantly decline. We want to be at the airport for an early departure.

That night, safe and sound in the privacy of my room is when I start to question what's happened. It's not that I doubt Jose's ability as a mechanic, but regarding aviation, I've always abided by procedures, and the idea to shorten the vent tube to fix the problem does not sit well with me. And what about the automotive oil and gasoline that was used to replace what was consumed in the first leg of the flight? I've been using auto gas in my airplanes for years with the difference that they're carbureted low compression engines and with a Supplemental Type Certificate (STC), which legally authorizes its use after meticulous field tests. This Mooney has an experimental fuel injection engine and there are no STCs that I know of that cover it for auto gas usage. I fall asleep with that disturbing thought. I don't sleep very well.

Chapter 44
Puerto Leguizamo

Day 3- Today, Sunday, December 30, 2012, 6:30 a.m. Puerto Leguizamo is blanketed with a light drizzle and the sky slightly overcast with sunrays trying to penetrate the layer. The vapor from the surrounding jungle is already present. I estimate the ceiling to be about 400 feet, not very good for flying over the jungle with an unpredictable engine. And what about the en route and destination weather report? What report? We haven't been able to contact Harry in Cali.

Well, for now, first of all, breakfast. The police escort drives us in their pick-up truck to the market in full swing at this time of the early morning. There are people everywhere queuing to get a sitting place at one of the many food stalls. All kinds of typical Colombian dishes are being cooked at once. I'm familiar with *arepas* and *almojábanas*, but the rest is unfamiliar to me. To accompany my coffee, I decide to try green plantain dough stuffed with pork rind and fried in a big cast iron pot. It looks good! However, after eating it, my conscience gets hold of me and I begin to regret having done it. It's far from the healthiest breakfast dish and not really the most recommended before a trip like the one we have ahead. But I did enjoy it.

As we're leaving the market, I suggest to Leandro that he buy a machete.

"For what?" he asks, obviously not familiar with this useful tool of the equatorial tropics.

"For whatever," I answer. I tell him that in Panama, the aeronautical authorities require that all aircraft carry one as part of the survival equipment. He looks at me cynically as he purchases one. So we walk out with a few oranges, bottled water and the machete or "sword" as Leandro and Jose jokingly call it, clueless as to how handy a tool it is.

Concerned about the characteristically autocratic mentality of the authorities throughout Hispanic America, I ask our escorts to drop me off at the Police Headquarters to get a letter from the chief stating why, when and how we arrived in Puerto Leguizamo and what our intentions are. The escort drops me off and continues on to the airport with Jose and Leandro. Getting the letter takes more than two hours; what with writing the letter and correcting the grammar several times on the computer; and a printer with no ink. They send for a printer in another office, but then they can't find the omnipotent official seal to stamp the letter. I wait patiently until the delay is resolved. Nothing changes in our latitudes. Could it be simply Spanish bureaucracy inherited from so many centuries past? I don't know, but I know for a fact that having a document with some kind of legitimacy is better than having nothing at all. Any official document that's stamped and authorized with a lavish signature commands respect.

Back at the runway, I find the airplane's top cowling removed and Jose and Leandro doing motor runs. I momentarily cringe. I don't like this panorama at all.

"And now what?" I ask them getting off the motorbike-taxi that brought me from town.

I'm informed that they had done a test with a transparent hose connected to the vent tube to observe the rate of any oil leakage. After running the engine for half an hour it started to leak again. So the shortened oil tube didn't work, and the fifteen-minute flight test yesterday was too short to determine that.

Jose proposes another alternative: Run the engine on reduced power to diminish the pressure in the crank case. Again, both convince me that it is a technically acceptable deduction, and I agree to a reduced power test flight of no less than one hour to determine exactly the loss of oil per hour and whether the flight can be completed without risks. I also insist that the flight be to Leticia instead of Tabatinga, where I know there are aviation shops that could check the engine out.

Leandro and I do the test flight, maintaining the power at 19 inches of manifold instead of the 28 inches we would normally use. We climb to 5,500 feet and fly circles over the airport. After an hour we land and check the oil consumption. We had only consumed half a liter of the twelve liters of oil. We extrapolate that in the three hours of flight that it would take us to fly to Leticia, we would only lose a liter and a half by venting and we would have ten and a half left in the reservoir. That settles it then, we're good to go!

But while Miguel goes for the quart of auto oil to replenish what was lost in the trials, it's already mid-afternoon and the weather shows signs of deteriorating. Under their protests, I make the decision to postpone the trip until tomorrow. Tabatinga, being our alternate, closes at six in the afternoon and that doesn't give us a sufficient margin of flexibility for possible deviations caused by bad weather en route or at our destination. We have no weather forecast to help in our decision-making, so the ruling to stay on the ground holds. I have to be firm on this because both are eager to continue and get home quickly, the beginning signs of Get-home-itis. Their desire to get going flaws their analysis of the situation. But as the pilot in command of this flight, even if it is only on paper, based on my criteria molded by experience, I exercise that power and I maintain the no-go determination.

Somewhat disappointed, we return to the same hotel, and to the same rooms, as we are the only guests. Since today is December 30, the hotel kitchen staff is preparing what will be served for tomorrow's New Year's Eve dinner: Roast pork, my all time favorite dish. I cajole the cook to prepare some pork rinds with green plantains, which we accompany with cold beer that we sent out for. For dessert, some ripe mangoes from the hotel patio tree. It's the first time that both Leandro and Jose have seen a mango tree, much less with mangoes ready for the picking. It's then that I realize that they're from another latitude, definitely not from our tropics.[44-A]

After such a distinctive treat, we go for a walk in town, for the first time without a police escort. The people are in a partying mood, the streets full of passers-by, motorcycles everywhere, dance music blaring out of each establishment, and the night is star lit. On the few occasions that I had to fly over Puerto Leguizamo and the one time we visited the town, it had never crossed my mind that it could be a town with as much activity as what I am seeing tonight. I don't know what the economy of this region is, since from the air one doesn't see agricultural fields or pastures for livestock; it's just a town surrounded by jungle next to a river. Its communication routes are by air, two Satena flights per week; and by river, fourteen hours upriver to Florencia or ten days downriver to Leticia. However, there are plenty of shops, restaurants, nightclubs and bars. I decide better not to speculate on the reason for this extraordinary boom.

Chapter 45
Jungle Haven

Day 4- December 31, 2012. It's a rainy day again with gray clouds and a gloomy overcast. We went to the market to have breakfast but this time I only ask for coffee with some corn *arepas*, having learned my lesson from yesterday's choice. At the market stall they recognize us and the service is fast and cordial. We're anxious to get to the airport. We don't want to welcome the New Year in Puerto Leguizamo.

Our police escort picks us up at the market and takes us to the airport where we meet Miguel, who, knowing of our plans to fly out early today, has come to offer his support services. While Leandro and Jose make the preparations to the plane, I review the route by extending the navigation charts on the plane's low wing and recalculating the times and fuel consumption. There is not much else I can do since I don't have wind reports at different altitudes, nor the weather forecasts en route or at our destination, that help a pilot in planning a flight. I'm so concentrated that I don't notice when Miguel approaches the airplane and begins to observe what I'm doing. He tells me that he's used to seeing maps with rivers, mountains and towns, but that the one I have spread out on the wing is totally undecipherable to him.

Patiently I explain to him that the lines can be compared with highways in the airspace for airplanes, and the numerical information gives minimum altitudes to safely cross over the terrain, while receiving navigational signals as well as airport information such as runway lengths and elevation and communication and navigation frequencies, all data related to the planning of a flight. He looks at the map carefully, and I see that he captures everything I explained. Then he asks me to indicate the route we will follow. So with my hand I trace a trajectory on the map from left to right, from one end to the other, to which he says: "Captain, do you know that between here and Leticia there is nothing but jungle? There are no airports or towns or anything on that route. The closest runway is well out of your trajectory, about sixty miles north."

I suddenly remember the map that I had brought from my hangar. It shows those details of this region, including rivers, international border limits and topographic information. I rummage through my travel gear and I pull it out. I spread it flat out on top of the wing and ask him, "Miguel, and are you familiar with the region?"

"Well, I was born and raised in Putumayo and I've been working at this airport for twenty-two years, and I hear the stories from the pilots who pass through here. Although I haven't been to any of those places, I know where they are. Araracuara is the only runway in this jungle between Puerto Leguizamo and Leticia. And it's deep inside the jungle, but it's in Colombian territory. Don't even think about entering Peru."

I know what Miguel is referring to about flying over Peruvian territory. In 2001, the Peruvian Air Force shot down a single-engine floatplane carrying a family of missionaries during a flight over the Amazon rainforest. The result of the investigation that led to this action came to light ten years after the event and involved anti-narcotics elements and agencies from the US and Peru. Conclusion: Hurried and lethal reaction without confirmation or identification of the aircraft. That knowledge of the incident is enough for me to take seriously and avoid crossing into Peruvian airspace at all costs.

"See if you can locate Araracuara on this chart."

Miguel studies the chart and starts to drag his finger across the chart from Puerto Leguizamo to Leticia and he says: "*Mire, Capitán*, here it is. Here's Araracuara, next to the Caqueta River that separates the Caqueta and Amazonas Departments. There's an army detachment there."

I circle the spot with my pen and I calculate the coordinates from the chart intending to program them later in the Mooney's GPS. At the same time, I notice that there's an ADF on site, and I jot down both bits of information in my flight notebook and slip it in my shirt pocket. I thank Miguel and I walk over to where Leandro and Jose are putting the engine cowling on and securing it.

I feel some misgivings in undertaking this flight because it's clearly not 100% within the safety or legality parameters. We haven't filed a flight plan, our permit to overfly Colombian territory has expired, we don't have en route or destination weather information or forecast, we're using fuel and lubricant not approved by the engine manufacturer, in short, a nerve-racking enterprise. Although we did carry out a one-hour test flight that revealed no anomalies, I'm not entirely at ease with that. At nine o'clock in the morning with a ceiling of broken clouds at 7,000 feet, we take off full of optimism and some misgivings on my part. But I'm aware that negligence and overconfidence are more dangerous than a deliberately accepted risk.

The climb is slow at this reduced power, but the morning is cool and that allows the plane to ascend effortlessly. It takes us thirty minutes to reach 5,500 feet. Now we're above of a layer of scattered clouds but with total ground contact. The Putumayo River on our right will accompany us for most of the journey. On the other side of the river is Peruvian territory. I don't take my eyes off the instruments, especially the oil pressure gauge. Everything is in the green, normal.

After settling at our cruising altitude for the trip, I try to contact any airplane flying in the area, but get no answer. Neither the control towers of Tres Esquinas nor Villavicencio or Amazonia Flight Center respond. There's no other option but to keep on going. It crosses my mind that nobody, except Miguel and the police escorts, know about our intentions, what time we took off, our route or even where we were going. Only the three of us know where we are at the moment. That's a thought that nags me.

Leandro is flying and listening to music on his iPod, but out of the corner of his eye he is staring at the instruments. Jose is sitting behind us and leaning forward, and he doesn't take his eyes off the instruments either. We've been flying for forty-five minutes and to keep busy and stop worrying about the instrument readings, I decide to enter Araracuara's coordinates in the GPS. Not completely familiar with this GPS, and because of its location in the instrument panel, to my left and below the dash, it's difficult to enter the letters and numbers: 00° 36' 06" S / 72° 24' 01" W. We're very close to the equator, the line that denotes the division between the northern and southern hemisphere. I have problems entering the coordinates correctly. I feel frustrated and decide instead to dial in the Araracuara ADF frequency: 453. I'm familiar with the equipment and in a matter of seconds it's done. Immediately the needle comes to life and points 90° to the left which means that at this precise moment we're abeam Araracuara. How far away, the ADF doesn't handle that information but I know it's a good 60-70 miles away. The instrument panel clock shows that we're an hour into the flight. Good, I guess.

Suddenly both Jose and Leandro notice a brief oscillation of the oil pressure gauge needle. They ponder if the oscillation is significant or not.

"Turn to the left and follow the ADF needle!" I shout immediately to Leandro. I see uncertainty in his face because I haven't given him any reason for that command. "The needle points to the nearest runway and we must get there immediately!"

"What runway? What are you talking about? We shouldn't divert from our route! Let's keep going on to Leticia," Leandro argues loudly.

"Yes, let's not leave our flight path," Jose intervenes. "Better we return to Puerto Leguizamo, it's closer than Leticia."

"No! We're closer to Araracuara. Just head there! Leandro, follow the ADF needle!" I insist emphatically.

Leandro reacts and turns the plane left following the ADF needle. In the cockpit, there's a sepulchral silence.

I again try to raise someone in all the area frequencies but to no avail. Nothing. I transmit in the blind on the international emergency frequency, 121.5, and still no reply. I select 7700, an emergency broadcast signal on the transponder hoping some radar site picks up our distress signal. Ten minutes have already passed. From the ADF we know in which direction Araracuara is, but that's all. We don't even know exactly where we are. If I had programmed the GPS in time, we would not be in this uncertainty. We would know where we are, the distance away from Araracuara and the time left to arrive; however, our predicament would still be the same: In trouble over inhospitable territory.

"Maintain the altitude until you see the runway. It must be next to a river in about twenty minutes," I tell Leandro calmly, as if I have everything under control.

"Abra Cadabra? Where did you get that information? How far are we from there?" Leandro asks.

"A-ra-ra-cua-ra. Talking to Miguel just before taking off. It is our only opportunity. We must be about twenty-five miles away now. Follow the needle."

I have a troubling feeling of doubt about all this. A river in the middle of the jungle, in this case the Putumayo River, while not a guarantee of survival, represents a thread of contact with something, a life line. But leaving it behind and flying deeper into the unknown doesn't do anything for reassurance. Jungle rivers characteristically have populations settled on their banks, but Miguel assured me that there's nothing in this stretch of the Putumayo River until it flows into the Amazon River at Leticia. Even with that dependable information, I feel like we're giving up some sort of protection by flying away, and what makes it worse, because of a decision I'm making.

All of a sudden, the engine starts to vibrate. Holy shit! Is the engine quitting? The three of us are stupefied. An engine usually gives a warning in one way or another that it's going to stop running, and this one has already given it twice: in David and in Puerto Leguizamo. This vibration is not a good sign. I instinctively slide the seat back to the maximum and tighten my seatbelt. I begin to secure all the loose objects on the instrument panel that could cause face damage in a sudden stop and tell Jose to do the same on the shelf at the back of the plane. I feel powerless at what's happening. It's strange, but I have no regrets about undertaking this trip. There's nothing more to do than wait and see what happens with the engine. An emergency landing in the middle of the jungle without anyone having the faintest idea where to start looking for us, or even that we're missing, doesn't make me feel good at all. I look down and see nothing but jungle. No towns, no rivers, no cattle, no roads, no trails. Suddenly, the engine starts to run normal again, no vibrating; it purrs smoothly.

"There's a river to the left," Jose yells out pointing straight ahead.

"Yes, that's the river, the runway must be parallel to the river. But follow the needle, direct," I call out with some relief.

"I see it, I see it!" Leandro exclaims as he prepares the plane for a landing, reducing power and lowering the landing gear and selecting 10° of flaps. He makes a left turn to align himself with the runway, but he's high and hot and when aligned on final approach, he decides to go around adding full power.

"What are you doing? No, no! Put it down; don't go around, the runway is long! Just sideslip it in!" I shout at him.

He ignores me and goes around to try another approach. Now, for the first time, I feel fear. By adding maximum power while turning around to approach from the other end of the runway, we're demanding too much from the ailing engine. This go-around will take two or three minutes, which can be crucial for this engine to continue running. The runway is surrounded by jungle and if we have to crash here, even if it's near the runway, finding us would be a matter of luck. That's if they were expecting us, which they aren't.

Why did he decide to go around in this critical situation? The flight path to the other end of the runway seems endless, but the engine is responding, although the needle is oscillating more than ever. Our only chance of survival is if the engine doesn't seize trying to get back to the runway. My breathing is slow and deep, my mouth is dry. It feels like it's full of cotton. I'm scared now.

Time has slowed down to a crawl. Seconds become minutes. I am acutely aware of everything below us. I remember reading that this effect, temporal distortion, is a perceptive phenomenon experienced when faced with life-threatening situations.

We're beginning the turn to align us on the opposite side of our initial approach when I see something that jars me out of the stupor and anxiety I've been under for the last moments. It's a beautiful waterfall in the middle of the river. It's as if destiny is giving me a magnificent spectacle before bringing me to the reality of the situation we're about to face. It soothes and calms me to the point where I am resigned to what happens. As we pass it, I turn my head to keep it in sight. Suddenly I feel the Mooney touching down, bouncing at high speed over the gravel runway and making a huge rattling noise. I feel the roar of the engine shut off, but I don't know if it's Leandro who's turned it off or if it just stopped by itself. I don't care. We're on the ground.

None of us say a word. After a few moments, I open the door and jump off onto the wing of the plane, followed slowly by Leandro and finally Jose. Our first sight is a derelict and depressing panorama. The runway is filled with mud puddles and surrounded by jungle. A group of armed men with automatic weapons and wearing camouflage approach us. There's a building that appears to be an abandoned hangar and several antenna towers next to a radar antenna and finally, watchtowers like those seen in concentration camps. What seems to be a 50-caliber machine gun protrudes from the nearest watchtower. Although Miguel had told me that Araracuara was a Colombian Army outpost[45-A], I ask myself: What if they're FARC?

Chapter 46
Acceptance and Determination

Day 4 continues- I scrutinize the uniforms and feel a welcome relief when I recognize them as Colombian Army. They immediately surround us and I believe they're more surprised than anything else. Right away the questions begin: Where do you come from? Where are you going? Why did you land here?

They seem to be questions more of curiosity than that of military protocol.

We ask them to help us push the Mooney toward a deteriorated concrete slab that appears to be the parking area. They jump in to help with enthusiasm, willing to do anything to break what seems to be the monotonous routine of guarding an airstrip in the middle of the jungle. The questions continue: How much does a plane like this cost? What country are you coming from? Where can I buy a watch like that? What make is it? How much does it cost?

The Jungle Infantry Battalion N-50 patch they wear on their uniform identifies their unit. Most seem to be no more than eighteen years old. Everyone wants to take pictures with us in front of the Mooney. After obtaining our identity information, the highest ranking soldier, a sergeant, leaves to inform his superior, the lieutenant in charge of the battalion. Soon, a crowd of civilians, and the ever present dogs appear out of nowhere attracted by the uncommon event: A never-seen-before civilian airplane with foreigners to boot. Again, the same type of questioning follows.

We're anxious to check the engine, so we courteously slip away from the crowd. When we check the oil-measuring rod, we find that the reservoir is empty, not a drop of oil. It's completely dry. We have lost twelve quarts of oil in an hour and a half of flight! How could this engine not seize from the lack of lubrication? Jose claims that in all his years as a mechanic, he had never seen or heard of an engine continue to run without lubricant.

An unannounced downpour makes us scatter for shelter, but after a few minutes, the sun is shining again, and the steamy air rises from the ground. The sergeant returns with instructions that we must follow him to the Battalion barracks to explain our presence to Lieutenant Higuera, the officer in charge while the major is on an official mission in Bogota. I propose that I go see the lieutenant while Leandro and Jose stay with the Mooney. On the way to the barracks, the empty aluminum cans that are hanging along the barbed wire fence surrounding the complex attract my attention. I realize it's a rudimentary measure to forewarn of the presence of intruders. Next we walk past one of the 30-foot high watchtowers where two on-duty soldiers standing next to their 50-caliber machine guns are staring down at me.

When we get to the main Battalion entrance, I have to wait outside until Lieutenant Higuera comes out. While there, I notice that every non-uniformed person who passes by the security post is body-searched and his documents scrutinized. I ask a soldier on guard duty about it.

"Well, look, this is a war zone, and there are a lot of guerrillas here and if you blink they can sneak in." He also tells me this is an obligatory path because the Devil's Canyon, a rocky and deep canyon, prevents continuous fluvial traffic through the river.

The Devil's Canyon! That was what I saw on the approach when I got that sense of resignation moments before landing. I make up my mind to look up more information on that spectacular canyon. It's got to have a history to it.

I suspect that the lieutenant's delayed appearance has to with his requesting instructions from the Battalion Central Command in Leticia. I notice antennas on the tall towers so I ask the soldier what they're for. He says they're for radio and cellular communication with the outside world. Even though I'm never invited to enter the compound, just watching the people hurriedly shuffling back and forth entertains me while I wait. I have a snapshot taken of me to remember the moment.

Lieutenant Higuera meets me just outside the fence, and I quickly explain our situation. He informs me that we're in a conflict zone and must abide by the Battalion regulations regarding security. He hands me three official documents with the Battalion logo, a macaw flying over the jungle. The documents detail the conditions for our stay here: Our movements are restricted to inside the complex and the landing strip, where the Mooney is parked. He's obtained accommodations for us at the Aero Civil radar station quarters and the Battalion will provide our meals while we solve our mechanical problems. We're locked down inside the complex between six in the afternoon and six in the morning. And finally, the note points out that the Colombian Army is not responsible if we're either injured, killed or kidnapped since this an area of conflict. Hmm, this is serious business.

I sign one of the documents and leave with the other two for Leandro and Jose to sign. I don't know what to make of what I just heard. We're being provided meals and a roof over our heads, but the idea of being in a conflict zone doesn't appeal to me. It's one thing to fly over war zones and another to be right in the middle of one. According to the lieutenant, in 2010, a detachment of ten policemen from Puerto Santander on the other side of the river in the Amazonas Department, was attacked and killed by the FARC on New Year's Eve; and from that day on, there's no police in the village. It's a settlement without authority, and since the army doesn't exercise police functions, more reason not to venture outside the restricted area.

When I get to the runway, I find Leandro and Jose making adjustments to the oil pressure pump. I stand and watch them for a bit, and then ask what's going on.

"By reducing the pressure in the crank case, it will prevent too much oil to be vented out," Leandro tells me with a smile. I'm stunned at what I'm hearing. These two are obviously still under the effects of a high dose of adrenaline from the recent scare. They're not reasoning well.

"And what oil do you think we're going to use, if we do not have a drop?" I ask, as if that question will make them desist from their unusual plan.

"We've been told that on the other side of the river, in Puerto Santander, they sell outboard motor oil, and we already sent word we'll be buying three gallons. And we have enough gas," Leandro replies smugly.

"Are you crazy or what?" I ask incredulously upon hearing even more foolishness. "That's the oil that's mixed with gasoline and used in two-stroke engines for lubrication, nothing to do with aviation engine oil. Nothing to do at all!"

"No, no, but listen, Ibu, besides that, we're going to replace the vent tube with a transparent plastic hose and snake it through a hole we'll make in the cowling so we can slide the hose through to the outside and monitor to see if oil leaks in flight. If the loss continues, we return; if not, we'll continue on."

With this last rationale, I react forcefully: "Just a minute, hold on! Let's reconsider for a second. We're in the middle of the jungle, in hostile territory, a war zone, with no flight plan, nobody knows anything of our whereabouts except us, and with an engine that's been letting us know that something's not right, and you two still think of continuing? What's wrong with you? This plane brought us safely here, and here is where we stay. Period. *No me jodan!*

I make a half turn and head to the other side of the runway and leave them alone, discussing the situation. After a while, Jose approaches me and tells me that they had considered what I've said and that yes, I'm right. We won't fly until either we have a new or reconditioned engine that replaces this one.

It seems unreal, but all this drama has been taking place in the few hours since we left Puerto Leguizamo this morning. We realize it's midday when we see the soldiers walking to the compound. They tell us that it's lunchtime. Actually, none of us, still affected by the near tragic experience, are hungry. We politely decline to accompany them. We stay by the airplane and discuss the options we have regarding the Mooney's engine. The motor must be sent for an overhaul, or a new one ordered. Either way, this motor has to be removed from the airplane. Two unknowns arise. Where do we send it, and how do we transport it there? The two soldiers ordered to remain with us hear us discuss the possibilities of whether to transport it via river either to Florencia or Leticia, both options unsafe and lengthy. Right away they jump in the conversation and inform us that the monthly supply flight coming from Bogota is soon to arrive, but they don't know when or what type of plane it is. They do agree it's big.

I inform Leandro and Jose about my meeting with Lieutenant Higuera and the impression I got of him being cooperative. We should ask him for assistance on the matter of transporting the engine out of here. I tell them I know of some first-class aviation engine workshops in Bogota. Both look skeptical, but I assure them and I'm certain of it since I personally have used them in the past overhauling my Cessna 140's engine. By having cellular and Internet communication, we'll be able to contact the Bogota repair facility for advice. Immediately I call my friend and Colombian pilot colleague Fernando Salazar, who is based in Panama, for his assistance in contacting the shop in Bogota. He establishes a link with the Aero Reparaciones in Bogota and asks them to contact us in Araracuara. For the first time since our dramatic arrival, I feel things are looking up. Thirty minutes later, Uriel, from Aero Reparaciones in Bogota calls to offers his support and cooperation in having the engine looked at. They can disassemble and inspect the engine and give us the diagnosis on whether it can be repaired or if a new one will be required. However, he tells us that tomorrow is the first day of the New Year, so throughout Colombia it's a holiday until January 3. New Year? In all this commotion, I didn't even remember it was December 31. What am I doing here in the middle of the Amazon rainforest on a day like today?

Chapter 47
Distorted New Year

Day 4 continues- The possibility of having an authorized facility check the engine allows us to prepare a work agenda to follow. First of all, we should talk to Lieutenant Higuera about getting the FAC supply plane to take us along with the engine to Bogota. I offer to handle that task while Jose will find out where there may be tools to remove the engine and propeller. Leandro will deal with moving our personal effects from the plane to our quarters.

Jose has gotten hold of a metal box full of general maintenance tools which will have to do for now. Walter, the Colombian Civil Aeronautics Directorate (DACC) technician assigned to the Araracuara communications and radar site has lent them to us. The DACC complex is located in a corner inside the military complex and surrounded by a cyclone fence. But the best news of all is that there's a tackle and chain rig and a steel A-frame that can serve to remove the engine from the fuselage. It's the only way since the engine with its accessories weighs over five hundred pounds. The A-frame will have to be disassembled to get it out the door of the building where it's located and the sections transported to the runway, where it can be erected on site and after using it, the procedure repeated in reverse. Of course, we'll need additional help because even when disassembled each section of the steel A-frame weighs over 150 pounds and there are a total of four. We'll deal with that tomorrow. Now the first thing is to remove the propeller. It takes us over two hours to remove it and carry it to the shed where it'll be stored until who knows when. I've done this before, so I know we've completed the easiest task of all. The most difficult will be removing the engine after disconnecting all the accessories, cables, wiring and linkages. I'll talk to the lieutenant to see if he can spare some soldiers to help us with the engine removal tomorrow.

We start to secure the plane, but again an unexpected heavy downpour drenches us, and we have to stop working until it stops. The rain is short but intense, but the mud it causes makes our work more difficult. It's already five o'clock and the mosquitoes begin to attack.

Between the stress of this morning's flight, the recurrent rain showers, the steam that's produced by the rain on the hot ground, in combination with the infernal heat, the challenge of removing and transporting the propeller, and the fatigue of not having had lunch, we're exhausted. The quarters assigned to us are in one of three concrete block buildings inside the military compound but without access to it: one enclosure inside another, the outer being the barbed wire perimeter fence. The sparsely furnished house consists of a living room, a kitchen and two bedrooms with three beds with old musty mattresses. There's a dining table but only one chair. The kitchen is devoid of everything. I got one of the bedrooms and Leandro and Jose the other. We'll have to bathe without soap and dry without towels. Nobody packed any. We thought we'd be staying in hotels throughout the trip. But then again, at this point, nobody's complaining, rather we're extremely grateful we don't have a jungle canopy for a roof and a layer of leaves for a mattress.

I find the DACC technician rather wary, but I guess

that's because he doesn't know who we are or what we're up to. I don't blame him. By rote, he explains the procedure to obtain our meals: We'll be handed our plates of food over the cyclone fence next to the soldier's mess hall. The plate, spoon and the cup issued are aluminum, and it will be our responsibility to have them available for each meal, washed and rinsed.

"Breakfast is at six, lunch at twelve and dinner at six. If you're not there on time, you won't eat," Walter warns us as he walks away towards a house I suppose is the assigned technician's quarters while on duty at this station.

We settle in our respective rooms and clean up before going for our meal. An air of gloominess is heavy with the thought of having to spend New Year's Eve in Araracuara. There's a piece of caked soap someone must have left in the shower ages ago, but we will still have to air dry our bodies. I find a hammock in the closet and take possession of it. Besides using it to dry off, I plan to sleep in it while I'm here in lieu of the cagy mattress. Minutes before six o'clock, we approach the cyclone fence and some of the soldiers recognize us and greet us. That simple, candid gesture makes me feel good. It must be that there's a certain affinity among those being trapped in the middle of this remote place. We eagerly wait for the aluminum plates to be hand-passed over the cyclone fence. A soldier who I assume is a cook's helper comes out of the mess with the plates.

"*Caballeros*, you're lucky to have arrived today. Today's meal is special being it's the last day of 2012. *Buen apetito.*"

It's drizzling and we start to run for shelter towards our quarters. As we pass by Walter's, he calls out from his doorstep for us to come over. It's a neat and more spacious house than ours, clean, with a well-equipped kitchen that includes a refrigerator and a stove. He offers his dining table for us to sit and plays the role of a good host. Grateful for the opportunity to eat sitting at a table with chairs, we settle for this last dinner of the year 2012: A double portion of rice, a large portion of yucca, a large portion of lentils, a small portion of canned tuna and *agua panela*, which is cane sugar syrup with water. I'll remember this last day of the year dinner as the most significant because of the mood I'm in at the moment, joyful and thankful for still being in this world.

During the meal, we get to know more about Walter and vice versa and the atmosphere relaxes. After a session of questions directed at us, it seems that he has accepted us as genuine persons in a predicament. He is a civilian DACC employee assigned to the Colombian Armed Forces specialized communications branch with responsibility for monitoring air traffic in this outlying sector of Caqueta and Amazonas where airborne narcotics and weapons trafficking prevails. He tells us drug trafficking flights originate in Bolivia and Peru and make scheduled stops at several points in the Colombian jungle, either for fuel or to unload the coca paste to be transported by river to the laboratories to be processed into cocaine. They've also detected flights that transport assault weapons that originate in Central America and are destined for the FARC's 48th Front that operates in the area. For that purpose, they have sophisticated communications and radar equipment operating in Araracuara. The first question I ask is if he had heard our transmissions on the international emergency frequency, 121.5 earlier, or if the radar had picked us up when we were transmitting on the 7700 emergency transponder code.

"Well, no. Today I shut down the equipment for generator maintenance. We were off the air."

A chill goes through my body as I realize that all odds were against us this morning while we were experiencing our emergency. All three of us look at each other in turn. Nobody, absolutely nobody knew anything about our whereabouts and much less about our predicament. Oblivious to the world in the middle of nowhere, that's where we were.

As soon as we finish our much-appreciated meal, our host informs us that within the enclosure of the outer perimeter fence there's a small store where they sell, among other things, beer. I feel that it's a sign that the party is over and that our host wants to be alone to prepare his New Year's festivities, mainly his dinner.

We quickly wash our utensils in his sink and head out to the store to celebrate the day's event: Safe and sound on the ground in Araracuara on this last day of 2012.

The Cuellar family store, located on this obligatory pathway between both ends of the Devil's Canyon, has a captive market. Unfortunately the beer is warm for lack of refrigeration and the celebration ends with only one beer apiece. We take a photo in commemoration and then retire to our quarters, each immersed in his own thoughts that I suspect are similar. Araracuara is not the place where any of us thought to welcome 2013.

As there is nowhere to put the hammock outside, I'm forced to sleep in the bedroom. I lay fully clothed and for a pillow I use my backpack and for a blanket, the hammock. I know that nights in the jungle are cold. As soon as I lie down and prepare to sleep, I start thinking about the events that have brought me here. I feel that chill again, the one I felt when the engine started vibrating this morning and I expected it to stop. At that moment I felt resignation but not fear. Why? Would it be faith in my guardian angel that my mother used to talk to me about as a child? I don't know, but what I do know is that I'm now having doubts about my actions that led me to this situation. There were several imprudent decisions that put me in this predicament, but at the same time, some of them were right. At least one, and that was to head immediately to Araracuara as soon as the emergency was detected. I mentally thank Miguel for that. Later I'll evaluate this flight calmly to learn from my mistakes and successes. It will all be registered in that little red book I've kept for more than forty years. In flying, one never ceases to learn.

All of a sudden, we hear loud explosions: Boom, boom, BOOM! What's the hell is that? Shit! Are we under guerrilla attack just as New Year's two years ago? I hurry out of the house where Jose and Leandro have already gathered and we can see soldiers on other side of the fence jumping up and down, yelling and screaming. We inquire what's going on. In the absence of fireworks, they're detonating mortars to celebrate the arrival of 2013. It's midnight. After the commotion dies down, I stay outside admiring the starry sky without a single cloud and again acknowledge that fate has dealt me a good hand.

Chapter 48
End of a Nightmare

Day 5 to Day 11- Exhaustion finally caught up with me that first dawn of 2013. I kept reliving the moment when the engine started vibrating and later, when Leandro decided to go around on short final. Those two scenarios kept playing over and over in my mind, but I did manage to sleep a few hours.

Suddenly my eyes open. Hey, it's almost six and breakfast will be handed over the fence in fifteen minutes! I find Leandro and Jose already awake and ready for breakfast, a piece of boiled yucca, a corn *arepa*, a lump of cane sugar and hot chocolate. Not bad, really, especially on this chilly morning.

After breakfast we organize ourselves to get the jobs before us completed: Disassemble the 20-foot high A-frame and carry the parts to the runway and reassemble it; remove the engine and transport it one way or another to the temporary storage until we sort out how to get it to Bogota. We'll definitely need additional labor, so I head out to the barracks to talk to Lieutenant Higuera about assigning some off-duty soldiers to help us and get an idea from him on how to get the engine and us out of here. I find the lieutenant inspecting the premises, and I approach him about hitching a ride to Bogota on the military transport. He promises to consult with the Army Command in Bogota about that possibility. The C-130 is scheduled to arrive on a supply run any day within the next two weeks with a day's notice. As for the assistance for today's jobs, he also agrees to get us a couple of off-duty soldiers to help us. I thank him and before leaving, I mention last night's mortar barrage.

He replies smiling with a smirk. "Oh that? We periodically discharge the mortar shells just to let the bad guys know we're here. You never know when they might pull something again." Shit. I wish he hadn't told me that.

When I return with the good news, Leandro and Jose have the A-frame already disassembled inside the generator house. Now comes the most difficult part, carrying the heavy pieces from here to the plane, about 550 yards away. Even though the frame has big castor wheels, it's not possible to roll it through this bog. We'll have to carry the disassembled pieces on our shoulders. Here the assisting soldiers come in handy. It's not until two in the afternoon that we finally get it re-assembled at the runway and attach the chain and tackle to lift the engine. Once we're able to lift the engine off the mounts, we lower it onto a makeshift pallet using extraordinary ingenuity from all present. At the absence of a wood saw, the machete we bought in Puerto Leguizamo is vital for cutting the pieces of wood used to make the pallet where the engine will remain waiting for transport to Bogota. When we finish the day's work, it's almost time for our last meal of the day, so tonight we'll get cleaned up after retrieving our meal over the fence. The meal tonight is noodles, lentils, sardines and a cup of *agua panela*. The good thing is that we've finished what we set out to do, and the bad thing is that we've finished what we set out to do. Now what to do with our idle days ahead until the Hercules C-130 transport arrives?

Not having anything pressing, we express our interest to Lieutenant Higuera to visit the Devil's Canyon. He agrees but sends two armed soldiers as escort. We don't complain about that, knowing what we know now about the bad guys. At the end of the runway, off to a side and almost swallowed up by the jungle, we discover the remains of a crashed Curtiss C-46. The soldiers know nothing about it when asked. It seems to have been abandoned decades before. We reach the canyon's edge and what we contemplate is spectacular: Below is an unrestrained current of turbulent water with its distinctive roar, rushing fast as it approaches the narrow junctures of the canyon. This is what I had seen from the air when I thought it was a divine gift offered me seconds before rendering accounts to the big guy in the sky.

After that half-day of exploring the surrounding area, we have no choice but to sit and wait for the C-130's arrival.

We wait for days, endless it seems, bored with nothing to do, captive in a military compound in the middle of nowhere. Our only reading materials are the Leticia Airport approach charts that I had obtained in Cali. To kill time, I decide to tutor Leandro with those approach charts. He grasps the procedures theory quickly, to the point that he memorizes all the information on the charts and to prove so, he practices in the yard walking through the depicted pattern and calling out the descent rates, minimums, decision heights and if he decides to miss the approach, he imitates the roar of the engine when applying maximum power. It's impressive to watch him drill over and over the procedure for Leticia's instrument approach. He has it memorized to the letter. At night, we discuss rules, regulations and restrictions applied to instrument approaches. He absorbs everything I can think of to tutor him.

On the fourth day, a civilian Air Colombia DC-3 arrives with supplies for Puerto Santander. Its next stop is Leticia. We consult among ourselves and decide that not knowing what the result of the engine inspection in Bogota might reveal, I might as well wait for the outcome in Panama rather than here. I could hitch a ride in the DC-3 to Leticia and from there, look for a way to return to Panama.

As I board the DC-3, guilt gnaws at me. I feel I'm abandoning my partners in adventure; but on the other hand, I'm very thankful to leave Araracuara behind.

Leandro and Jose remained waiting for the much-announced Hercules C-130 to arrive. At the end of eleven days it landed with the supplies for the outpost and flew them and the engine to Bogota, where it was taken to Aero Reparaciones for inspection. The overhaul took three weeks, and Leandro and Jose remained in Bogota the whole time. According to Uriel, the engine was in terrible condition from not having flown for over three years before embarking on this challenging trip. All the internal moving parts of the engine, in addition to the cut oil tube, were replaced. It was bench tested for hours under maximum power settings and certified ready to operate.

The transfer of the repaired engine to Araracuara was an adventure I missed. Leandro told me that they contracted a freight truck to take them from Bogota to Villavicencio, on the other side of the mountain. They were part of a caravan of vehicles, which is the norm for traveling on roads that traverse desolate sections of the country. Halfway there, the caravan was detained by an alleged FARC patrol, but they may well have been common armed bandits. The freight truck they were in was third in line behind two buses full of passengers, who were stripped of all their valuables by the highway bandits. Once satisfied with their loot, they waved the truck by. Their interest was in the private vehicles following that promised bigger profits than a dilapidated freight truck. The driver kept repeating how lucky they had been not to be detected as foreigners, since the ransom the bandits could have demanded for their release would have been substantial. According to Leandro, that scare was almost as bad as the one they had experienced weeks before in the ailing Mooney. Almost, but not quite!

Above: Leandro, Jose and Ibu in Cali, Colombia, preparing for the flight to Tabatinga, Brazil.

Above 1: Leandro and Jose dressed for tropical heat, under police inspection. Puerto Leguizamo, Putumayo, Colombia.
Above 2: Landing strip in the military complex, Araracuara, Caqueta, Colombia.
Above 3: Ibu with the damaged Mooney escorted by soldiers from the Selva N-50 Infantry Battalion.

Above: Ibu with the machete that saved the day, accompanied by members of the N-50 Battalion.

Below: Dismantling the Mooney's motor.

Above 1: Ibu in the armed conflict zone. Caqueta, Colombia.

Above 2: The DC-3 that transported Ibu to Leticia, Amazonas, Colombia.

Adrenaline Overdose 319

Above: Leandro and Jose in front of the Devil's Canyon, the border between Caqueta y Amazonas, Colombia.

Epilogue

After that failed trip to Bahia Blanca, Argentina, my flying activity is now devoted mostly to maintaining and flying my Cessna 140A, a small two-place taildragger manufactured in 1951. In 1990, I found this classic in a deplorable state of neglect in Paitilla airport. It belonged to a USAF colonel assigned to Howard AFB. He had acquired it with the intention of restoring it back to life, but after being riddled with bullets during the US invasion in December of 1989, and cannibalized in the chaos that ensued for days after, he decided to sell it as is, where is. The plane had the original logbooks where I discovered it had an impressive history. It had left the factory directly for the Salvadoran Air Force, where they used it for training pilots for several years before it was sold in Guatemala, and then resold in Costa Rica where it was also used for instruction. From Costa Rica it was brought to France Field, Panama. It had had several owners who flew it all over the countryside. How could I, knowing of its trajectory, allow this relic to be lost? I acquired it from Colonel Gates and proceeded to make it fly again. With the help of Isaac Martinez, a Changuinola mechanic friend, we got it back in the air within a year.

Despite having the opportunity to fly other more modern and impressive aircraft, the 140 has remained a faithful and noble companion for more than twenty-five years. Now its use is limited to personal transportation and to introduce aspiring pilots to aviation, allowing me to give back much of what I received from other aviators over the years. It also keeps my flying skills tuned.

I recognize that I've been fortunate to have been exposed to aviation during a time when things were uncomplicated and practical. The access I had to planes, pilots and airports fueled that enthusiasm. My career in aviation has been a passion ignited from the beginning, and it ended in the type of flight tailor-made for me in Evergreen: No set itineraries or established routes; exotic destinations and some never-heard-of places; unconventional passengers and cargo and purposeful flights; and lastly, total satisfaction before, during and after each flight.

Would I have liked to be in command of a sophisticated and modern airliner? Of course, what pilot doesn't dream of it! Moreover, I have admiration and respect for those who have reached that peak in aviation. But the regimented and routine path of an airline pilot at best would have kept me from that independence and that uncharted future I fully relished.

I'm proof that dreams do come true. That night, flying over the Magdalena, I recognized that I had arrived, that I was where I always wanted to be, doing my thing. But to arrive doesn't mean the end of the journey. My logbook, though thick with nine thousand hours, has room for more.

Above: Ibu at the controls of an Air Panama 727.

Below: Ibu and Captain Billy Earle in Tocumen Airport after flying the B-727.

Right: The instructor, Captain Isauro Carrizo, being checked out by Ibu, his ex-pupil. 2017.

Notes

Chapter 1: First Memories

[1-A] Ground effect – When an aircraft flies close to the ground, the wing lift is increased due to the downward displacement of the air mass, resulting in a force in the opposite direction, upwards. Pilots operating on short runways use this effect to force the plane to fly before its time. Upon reaching the end of the available ground strip, full flaps are briskly applied, causing the plane to balloon and remain flying at a slow speed over the ground. As the speed increases, the flaps are slowly retracted to enable the plane to climb. Even though not found in any airplane operations manual, it's a proven effective maneuver utilized worldwide.

[1-B] Critical engine failure on takeoff – The DC-3 Lacsa pilot faced a power imbalance when his left engine failed on take-off. This caused the plane to swing to the left where the power had been lost. The pilot immediately aborted the takeoff at the same time keeping the aircraft from veering off the runway to the left, and stopping before the end of the runway. Because the DC-3 has the directional wheel at the tail, during this unbalanced power emergency, greater skill on the part of the pilot is required in order to control the airplane as opposed to an airplane with the steering wheel on the nose.

Chapter 2: A World Apart

^{2-A} The Douglas Aircraft Company first launched the DC-3 in 1937. The original version was a passenger model but later, when WWII loomed, it was built in the military configuration and designated as the C-47. This version had a reinforced floor and a strengthened fuselage to permit a larger entrance cargo door. Most of the DC-3s that operated in Panama were C-47s, which could easily be utilized for both cargo and passengers. Both versions are commonly referred to as DC-3s.

Chapter 3: El Campo

^{3-A} Abaca is a plant of the Musa genus (*Musa textilis*) similar to the banana family. Its leaf-stem is used to make Manila hemp.

^{3-B} Marcos A. Gelabert – In Justo Arroyo's book *Corazón de águila*, he states that the UFCo in Costa Rica employed Gelabert as a pilot during the Second World War years, 1941-1945, when non-military aviation was banned in Panama for Canal security reasons. This makes it possible that Gelabert was the pilot of that flight.

Chapter 4: Airport Recollections

^{4-A} James Red Gray – Ex-World War II US pilot who settled in the Chiriqui province and was part of the aviation boom during the 1960s. He is known for accompanying General Omar Torrijos on the last leg of the flight from Mexico to Panama, after a military insurrection by other National Guard officers in 1969 attempted to remove him from power.

Chapter 5: Aeronautical Development

[5-A] Paitilla – Name used to refer to the airport located in the Paitilla area, Panama City since 1929 and renamed Marcos A. Gelabert Airport in 1952. When the "Paitilla" airport was closed in 1999, Albrook Field in the former Canal Zone was opened and renamed Marcos A. Gelabert when operations were moved there on January 1, 2000.

Chapter 8: The Bug Bites

[8-A] Ground loop – In aviation there are two types of land planes: conventional and tricycle gear. The ground loop is associated with conventional aircraft, or "tail wheel" aircraft. Since the center of gravity is behind the main gear, while moving on the ground, either taking off or landing, the tail end tends to rotate in a horizontal plane towards the front. If this trend isn't counteracted immediately, control of the plane may be lost and the wing drops toward the ground, which can cause damage to the propeller, the landing gear and the wingtip, as well as the pilot's ego.

[8-B] Stick and ball – Basic flight instrument that indicates if the airplane is flying in a coordinated manner, and is consulted often by the pilot especially in turns. The ball in the center affirms it.

Chapter 9: Pheromones in Flight

[9-A] Three-Point Landing – When a conventional airplane lands on all wheels simultaneously, the main gear wheels and the tail wheel.

Chapter 14: Unconventional Check Airman

14-A The Left Seat – In a two-pilot cockpit, traditionally the pilot-in-command sits on the left side. The single-pilot aircraft designed at the beginning of the 20th century had a rotary engine, and the torque produced by the engine made turning to the left easier than turning to the right. When airplanes were designed with two seats side by side, the seat on the left was exclusively for the captain. That side had the engine instruments and navigation equipment, and it also offered greater visibility during turns to the left that were assumed to be more frequent, taking into account that the standard landing circuits were, and still are, to the left. Later, in the beginning of commercial aviation, navigation to travel from one point to another tended to follow railways or roads. The aircraft were kept on the right side of the line, so the opposite traffic was passed on the left side. Again, being located on the left side was an advantage. Once aviation was regulated, it was established that the procedure to avoid a head-on collision between two planes would require a right turn by both to avoid collision, a procedure inherited from the Right of Way Rule of the sea. The pilots-in-command, sitting on the left side, would have a better visibility of the other plane and be able to evaluate the situation more effectively. Even today with aircraft that have jet engines, where torque is not a factor, the left seat is reserved for the pilot-in-command.

Chapter 15: Back Seat Jockey

15-A Flight Simulator – Flight simulators artificially simulate the flight of an aircraft accurately and are used extensively to train pilots. In addition to eliminating the danger of practicing maneuvers and emergency procedures in real flight, it expedites and reduces the cost of training crews for airlines. The first was designed and put into operation in 1929 by Edwin Link, and used for military training from the beginning, but it wasn't until 1934 when the FAA approved it for civilian pilot training. United Airlines was the first commercial airline to use it as a training tool in 1954.

Chapter 16: Cloud Seeding

[16-A] Cloud Seeding – In short, during cloud seeding particles of salt or dry ice or other chemical components such as silver iodine are introduced into a cloud to stimulate precipitation. It's a process that, according to its detractors, has not been scientifically proven as effective.

[16-B] Pressurization – Aircraft with pressurized cabins have a system that maintains atmospheric pressure at a level equivalent to 6,000 to 8,000 feet above mean sea level when flying at higher altitudes, allowing crews and passengers not to have to wear oxygen masks.

[16-C] Hypoxia – Hypoxia is caused by the lack of sufficient oxygen in the blood to maintain a normal physiological function. In aviation, the most common cause of hypoxia is flying more than 30 minutes in non-pressurized aircraft at more than 12,000 feet during the day or 10,000 feet at night without supplemental oxygen. Fatigue and euphoria are the first detectable signs, followed by an impediment to perform simple manual and mental tasks. Hypoxia is painless and the danger is that the signs and symptoms can develop gradually and could be established before the person affected realizes it. The final result of hypoxia is the loss of consciousness.

Chapter 27: In the Air Again

[27-A] Electric system of a piston aircraft – Once the engine is running, the generator or alternator kicks in to supply current to the electrical system through the battery. It also restores the battery charge lost during the start, while the voltage regulator maintains that load in a specific operating range. If there is damage or failure in the electrical system in flight, the engine operation is not affected; the engine produces its own electricity through its magnetos, which provide the spark to the plugs that cause the detonations in the cylinders. These detonations or explosions move the pistons that rotate the crankshaft coupled to the propeller, which it turns. A failure in the electrical system would only affect the communication, navigation and lighting systems, but even so, the battery would supply the electric current for a certain time, depending on its hours-amperage capacity.

Chapter 34: Captain's Stripes

[34-A] Operational ceiling – For a piston aircraft this is the altitude where it can still ascend at a maximum rate of 100 feet per minute. For jet engine aircraft it is 500 feet per minute. The absolute ceiling for any aircraft is the maximum altitude where an aircraft can maintain level flight and where its rate of climb is reduced to zero.

Chapter 36: Recruitment and Training

[36-A] Plan Colombia – Initially Plan Colombia was a diplomatic project proposed by Colombian President Andres Pastrana and accepted by President Bill Clinton in 1998 to fight drug cartels in Colombian territory with US support. The Plan was implemented in 1999 with a clear vision of creating an anti-cocaine strategy. With time it became reliant on military support to end the armed conflict in Colombia. Critics of the initiative argue that the Plan did not prosper given the marked influence of right-wing paramilitary groups in the Colombian Army. Aerial spraying to eradicate coca crops was also questioned because of claims that the application of glyphosate herbicide was harmful to people, animals and all crops. The official arguments in favor of the aerial applications were that because the FARC had concealed land mines in the coca fields, glyphosate aerial applications prevented deaths and injuries to the soldiers entrusted to manually pull out the plants by the roots. Some circles consider that the Plan played a decisive role in pressuring the FARC to a dialogue with the Colombian government and to the peace agreement in 2016 ending the 52-year armed struggle.

[36-B] Runway Touchdown Zone Markings – The markings on the runways vary depending on the use or type of runway. In the case mentioned during the ATP check-ride in Atlanta, the examiner expected me to touch down in the delineated area (Runway Touchdown Zone Marking) 500 feet from the threshold. This area is defined with two parallel white broad rectangles to the side of the center of the runway. I touched down right at the beginning of the threshold. That definitely was not what the examiner was looking for. I failed that check-ride.

Chapter 37: Getting Acclimatized

37-A Information on the tragedy of the Curaray River – Two films were made of this tragedy: *End of the Spear* and *Beyond the Gates of Splendor*. By way of interest, the film *End of the Spear* was filmed largely in Panama. The river scenes that supposedly are of the Curaray River in Ecuador were taken on the Chagres River upstream from Lake Alhajuela. Jaime Fabrega M. was the pilot flying the filming crew in a Helix SA Bell Jet Ranger Helicopter. *https://en.wikipedia.org/wiki/Operation_Auca*.

Chapter 39: Mexican Stopover

39-A JB – After leaving EHA, JB was contracted to fly in Afghanistan for a US military contractor. The plane he was flying one night disappeared from radar coverage, but the details of the official investigation have yet been made public. There are indications that it could have been a collision with a drone.

39-B Scopolamine – This drug is derived from a tropical plant, and when assimilated by the person, produces immediate memory loss and a total submission for several hours or even days. It's usually provided through food and drinks, and through inhalation. In addition to loss of memory, the person's will is dulled and is therefore left vulnerable to manipulation. This narcotic is known in Colombia and Mexico as *Burundanga*, and *Aliento del diablo* (Devil's Breath).

Chapter 40: Mission Rejected

40-A On February 13, 2003, the FARC captured three Plan Colombia US civilians, Keith Stansell, Marc Gonsalves, and Tom Howes, after their Cessna Caravan C-208 suffered mechanical failure and they were forced to land. Pilot Tommy Janis and the Colombian liaison, Sergeant Luis Alcedes Cruz, were executed on site. The book Out of Captivity, authored by the three ex-captives describes the ordeal in detail.

Chapter 41: End of a Saga

41-A Brad – Brad was determined to get into the Colombian soap opera world as an actor. He had already made positive contacts in the industry right before EHA operations ended. Eventually he did get to act in the TV series *Dangerous Flights*. Brad died of cancer in 2013.

41-B Narco-submarine – The Tumaco narco-sub measured 60 feet in length, had the capacity to carry 10 tons of cocaine and had a speed of 18 knots and was driven by diesel engines. The crew consisted of four persons. The cost of manufacturing one of these submarines is estimated at two million dollars, but the value of the cargo could surpass four hundred million dollars. The captured submarine's range was 2,000 nautical miles. The construction materials consisted of plywood and fiberglass and to navigate, it used a portable over-the-counter GPS and a periscope. The breathing air for the crew was through a PVC vent tube. The trip from the Colombian coast to the Panamanian, Central American or Mexican coast takes between three to seven days. The payment for a successful cocaine-laden trip is so lucrative that volunteers to crew them abound. There are no statistics of the effectiveness or loss at sea of these submarines, but the Colombian naval authorities estimate that more than half don't reach their destination.

Chapter 44: Puerto Leguizamo

44-A Tropical region – The Tropics, also known as the Torrid Zone, is the region included between two parallel latitudes: 23.5° N (Tropic of Cancer) and 23.5° S (Tropic of Capricorn).

Chapter 45: Jungle Haven

45-A Araracuara – Officially known as The Penal and Agricultural Colony of the South, it was once the most feared prison in Colombia. It operated from 1937 to 1971 in Araracuara, on the border of Caqueta and Amazonas Departments, in the heart of the Amazon jungle. Its access is limited partially by boat on the Caqueta River or by air. According to its history, the inmates used hammers and chisels to carve the rock slabs to make the runway. After being abandoned as a penal colony, guerrillas and drug traffickers used this colony to imprison hostages during ransom negotiations, and the runway was used for drug planes to refuel on their trips north. In 2003, the Colombian Army together with the US Army closed this strategic corridor to illegal armed groups, forcing them to retreat deeper into the jungle. Today the Colombian

Army heavily guards this site.

Note: YouTube has a video of a DC-3 (HK 3286, formerly Copa's flagship HP-86) overflying the Devil's Canyon in an approach to Araracuara's runway: *DC-3 arrival Araracuara, Caqueta, Colombia.*

Books about Aviation in Panama

Alvarado, Pat. *Vuelo épico * Epic Flight*. Piggy Press Books, 2012.

Armbruster, Edwin D. *Unusual Attitudes*. Xlibris, LLC, 2014.

Arroyo, Justo. *Corazón de águila*. La Boina Roja, 1996.

Burdne, Maria Schell. *The Life and Times of Robert Fowler*. Borden Publishing Company, 1999.

Carrizo, Isauro. *Grandes personajes de la aviación panameña*. Imprenta Universitaria, 2012.

Carrizo, Isauro. *Historias cortas de la aviación*. Editora Sibauste S.A., 2009.

Hagendorn, Dan. *Alae Supra Canalem*. Turner Publishing Company, 1995.

Hagendorn, Dan. *Conquistadors of the Sky*. University of Florida Press, 2008.

Kursen, William A. *Flying the Andes*. University of Tampa, 1997.

Martínez, José de Jesús. *Teoría de vuelo*. Centro de Educación Educativa, 1979.

Sarasqueta, Germinal. *Aeropuerto de Paitilla*. Aero Publicaciones, 2003.

Sarasqueta, Germinal. *De la carreta a la avioneta*. Aero Publicaciones, 2014.

Sarasqueta, Germinal. *Inmortales de la aviación panameña*. Aero Publicaciones, 2012.

Sarasqueta, Germinal. *Momentos memorables de la aviación panameña*. Aero Publicaciones, 2013

Toral, Octavio M. *El comienzo de la aviación en la*

República de Panamá. 1999.

    Véliz, Moisés. *Alas cordiales.* 2001.

    Véliz, Moisés. *Copa en el siglo 21.* Panamericana Formas e Impresos S.A., 2012.

Acknowledgments

Many contributed to make this book as close to the events that appear here. I owe thanks to the following people: Elsie Howard and captains Guillermo Billy Earle and Miguel Mike von Seidlitz, who lived the years of the aviation apogee in Changuinola, for helping to refresh my memory and clarifying certain historical concepts. I owe special thanks to Captain Earle for reviewing the manuscript in detail. Clyde Stephens, Carlos Medina, Dania Rivera and pilots Nemesio Ledesma and Tam Syme contributed with verification of dates, data and photographs of the beginning of aerial spraying in Changuinola. Gustavo Tato Cuervo, from my initial days of training in Paitilla, was consulted repeatedly. Bolivar Chaparro Serrano shared his immense memory of events and characters of the time. The authors of the publications that appear at the end of the book, that when reading them, encouraged me to continue writing. And finally, the project would not have been finished without the push and dedication of the editor of Cecropia Press, Pat, my wife and companion on many of these adventures since the beginning, for diagramming, editing and publishing this book. My gratitude for keeping me focused.

LAK, 2017

The Aviator
Luis A. Alvarado K.

At the early age of five, Ibu's fascination with aviation began, and that fascination has not diminished over the years. His entry into the real world of aviators commenced right after his college graduation, a journey of continued and persistent dedication to flying. This narration of camaraderie, humor, jolts and some severe realities make for a complex look into the mind of a true aviator.

Cecropia
Press

cecropiapress.com

www.ingramcontent.com/pod-product-compliance
Lightning Source LLC
LaVergne TN
LVHW041330080426
835512LV00006B/391